Adoption:
My Salvation

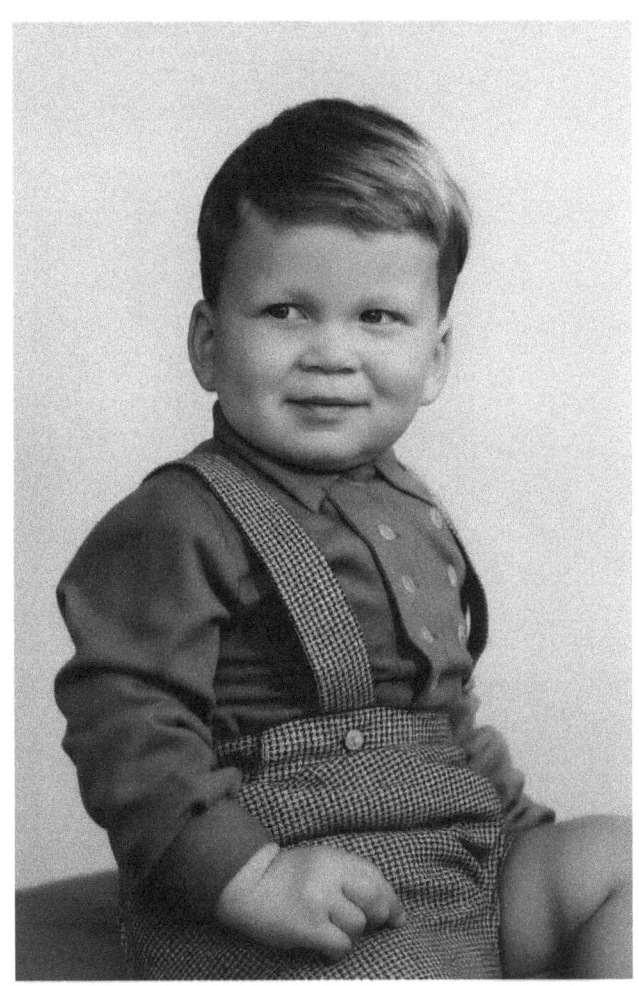

Jon Carter

Acknowledgements

This book is dedicated to my wonderful parents, Joyce and Dennis, who adopted me when I was six months old. Thank you, Mum and Dad.

Wedding Day

I would also like to thank:

My best friend, Tracy Wiffen, for her unswerving loyalty and support, Sarah Woods, forever my soulmate, Steven Knight, there for me in my hour of need. My great mate Jim O'Brien, Clarissa Young, and Eleanor Barlow, Staff at Marriot Lodge Care Home, for taking care of my dear Mother.

Prologue

My journey began in 1958 at 39 Woodland Way, Morden, in Surrey. Adopted at six months of age, I was starting life with my wonderful parents Joyce and Dennis, who selflessly took the decision to adopt a child and give me a chance.

The family home was a three-bedroom terraced house with neat gardens front and rear, set in a leafy road with fine manicured verges and trees, very picturesque. The town centre boasted many shops and a cinema, it was busy and thriving. Green open spaces nearby included Morden Park and Morden Hall Park, the latter incorporating Morden Hall which was built in the 18th Century. With Hillcross infants and Junior school a few minutes walk away, together with St James' Church nearby in Martin Way, it all made for a friendly and welcoming neighbourhood. St James' played a huge role in my life. I was christened and baptised there, joining the Church of England.

The history of Morden dates back to ancient times with evidence of Roman roads and Saxon settlements. Agriculture was the main theme amid a rural village setting. Major landowners, including the Garth family, played a significant role in shaping the landscape and development of Morden. The River Wandle and Morden Mills were important for milling and other industries. Inter-war years saw the rise of housing estates and a more urban environment, and in 1965 Morden became part of the new London Borough of Merton.

My Mother was raised in Battersea, London at 20 Winders Road, living there with her sister Doris and their mother Edith, my grandmother. Mum worked as a bank clerk and was a member of the Mother's Union.

The Union was founded in 1876 and is a Christian charity, encouraging parents to bring up children in the faith and life of the Church. Mum was an exceptional cook and keen gardener, knowing the names of every flower and she had a wicked sense of humour. Winders Road is known for its residential character and dates back to Victorian and Edwardian times. There was a dramatic increase in terraced housing from the 1850's onwards, resulting in a predominantly residential setting.

201 Gander Green Lane in Sutton, Surrey was the birthplace of my Father, where he lived with his Dad Arthur, my Grandfather. Their house was opposite Sutton United football ground, the site originally being open fields and allotments in the 19th century. Development as a football arena came about during the Edwardian period.

My Father worked for the Post Office (now British Telecom) from the age of 14. He began as a post-boy and worked through the ranks to head of Group for Traffic Division. Dad was very calm and unflappable, an accomplished pianist and organist. He used to cycle between Sutton and Battersea to court my Mother. How wonderfully old-fashioned that was. Sutton was formerly a Saxon settlement and small farming village until the 19th century. The railway revolutionised the area in 1847, and the most ancient relics can be located at St Nicholas Church.

Adoption was a taboo subject during the 1950's and 60's, single parents were frowned upon and often treated in a cruel fashion for bearing a child out of wedlock. The adoption process can be complex and lengthy. To begin with, prospective parents research agencies and select one to suit their needs. A panel reviews the details of the applicants, and once approved, the agency works to locate a suitable child. After a match is found, the parents then meet the child. Then, after all the legal procedures are met, an adoptive family is established.

So, there I was, secure in a happy family environment living in Morden. I feel blessed that my parents chose me, and I will be forever grateful. There were many experiences and adventures ahead, a varied and complex life lay in wait!

Table of Contents

Acknowledgements i
Prologue iii
CHAPTER 1 A New Beginning 1
CHAPTER 2 Liberation 12
CHAPTER 3 Transformation 23
CHAPTER 4 A New Decade 29
CHAPTER 5 Independence 37
CHAPTER 6 Dark Moments 46
CHAPTER 7 New Challenges 51
CHAPTER 8 Personal Development 59
CHAPTER 9 Tragedy 65
CHAPTER 10 Protecting Mum 73
CHAPTER 11 Global Crisis 82
CHAPTER 12 On The Brink 85
CHAPTER 13 End of an Era 89
Summary 95

CHAPTER 1

A New Beginning

My earliest recollection was as a toddler, aged two, with an inquisitive nature and full of mischief. Our neighbour, Mrs. Gill, often called round for a coffee and a chat. She was a statuesque lady and wore floral dresses and a grey cardigan, typical fashion of 1960. One day, when she and Mum were talking, I explored

the cupboard under the stairs and discovered my father's shoe polish. I then smeared it all over my white romper suit! 'What a cheeky chappie Jon is,' remarked Mrs. Gill. 'That is one way to describe him,' replied my Mother. On his return from work, my Dad always got it in the neck; it was his fault!

I gradually learnt to walk and talk, taking in the big, wide world in front of me. By the time I was four, in 1962, there was a new addition to the family: Jay, our brown and white Springer spaniel.

A year later, my education began at Hillcross Infants and Junior School, a few minutes walk from our home. The facility was set in spacious grounds with large playing fields, a leafy copse

set in one corner. A concrete playground ran adjacent to the classrooms. It was a new and strange experience, a really big deal for a five-year-old. I was introduced to my teacher, Miss Field, a portly lady who wore pleated skirts and heavy brown shoes, her grey hair in a bun, steel-rimmed glasses perched on her nose. A boy in my class had the same surname as me, so Miss Field referred to me as J.C., my nickname that stands to this day.

During an arithmetic lesson, she asked, 'Who knows what 3 x 7 equals?' I raised my hand and replied, '21, Miss Field!' She smiled and said, 'Well done, what a clever boy you are, JC!'

As time progressed, I was appointed milk monitor. I did not know what that meant, but I was given a badge, so it felt important! Sports were fun, I got into football, and Dad bought me a pair of boots. I was the envy of the school! He taught me to clean them with Dubbin and keep them that way. In 1965, Dad took me to watch Sutton United, very special given the family connection to that area. I was open-mouthed with excitement, my first of numerous visits to a football arena.

During the same year I joined the choir at St. James', our local church, where I had been christened and baptised. Inaugurated in 1958, St. James' is a splendid building located in Martin Way, Morden.

My Father was organist and choirmaster there for more than thirty years, and I used to stand next to the organ after Sunday morning service and just watch him play. A gifted pianist, a wonderful, talented man, and always smart in a shirt and tie.

It transpired that I had a great soprano voice; a star was born! Some boys at school made fun of it, I did not let them bother me, my pride took care of that. On reaching the age of ten, an invitation to train at the Royal School of Church Music (RSCM) had arrived. The RSCM was located at Addington Palace near Croydon, in Surrey, with rooms for many boarders and spacious grounds for sports and exercise. The concept was to form a 'special choir' to support the Westminster Abbey choir in a recital of 'The Passion,' by J.S. Bach.

THE PASSION
according to Saint Matthew

J. S. BACH
(Abridged Version)

Sung by
WESTMINSTER ABBEY CHOIR
and
WESTMINSTER ABBEY SPECIAL CHOIR

NOT TO BE TAKEN AWAY

There were many boys from all over the country gathered at the school. I represented my church amongst the throng. My stay there was for a week. We conducted various rehearsals of hymns and psalms. Dad popped in every evening, which was a great comfort. I had never been away from home before. Eventually, the list was whittled down to the final twelve, and I was selected to be a member of the 'special choir', a great honour indeed.

There were ten rehearsals on consecutive Monday evenings at Westminster Abbey, the most famous church on the planet, which has stood there since 1066. My Father accompanied me for each rehearsal and was bursting with pride. The conductor was Mr. Douglas Guest, a fearsome-looking man but with a heart of gold. He was world-famous, six feet tall, in a smart suit and tie, always sweating, often combing his black hair.

At the start of each session, we practiced our scales, 'doh-ray-me' etc, up and down. Mr. Guest looked at me and said, 'Carter, sing your scales, please, and not too loudly, it has to be controlled.' 'Yes, sir,' I replied and duly obliged. He looked happy enough. The weeks passed, and we practiced and rehearsed 'The Passion' until we knew it in our sleep. The recital was drawing near, and excitement was growing. The final dress rehearsal arrived, and it was seamless; we were now ready.

I recall how calm I felt as the 'Special choir' filed into the choirstalls, positioned in front of the main Abbey choir. This was the pinnacle for all choirboys. My parents were in the congregation, beaming smiles on their faces.

Amongst the dignitaries present was the Duchess of Kent, together with ladies in their finery and smartly suited gentlemen. Both choirs sang 'The Passion' perfectly. The whole service was wonderful, Mr. Guest exemplary. At the conclusion, I recall the relief and exhaustion in his demeanour, a privilege to be conducted by him. It had been a great day at the Abbey, a building steeped in so much history.

This great event was the talk of our church. I was so proud of my achievement, as were my parents. My dear Father taught me so much about the art of singing, the volume, tempo, breathing techniques, all of it. It was thanks to Dad that I sang at the Abbey. Then a few weeks later, at evensong, something strange happened to me. My voice broke! One minute I was soprano, then bass! My angelic tones had lasted just long enough for the recital, what a relief. Dad said, 'Well, it looks like you will be in the back row with the old chaps now!' I laughed and replied, 'That's fine Dad, I was so proud to be a soprano, thank you for teaching me so well.' We had a hug and laughed together. Mum quipped, 'Jon, a beard and a pipe are the order of the day now, you will blend in perfectly.'

My Mother always had a great sense of humour, one of her greatest traits. Forever a cheeky glint in her blue eyes, ready for the next one-liner!

Later the following year my Father took me to a game at Wimbledon Football Club, as I was crazy about the sport by then. Set in Plough Lane, London SW19, the stadium was huge compared to Sutton United. Wimbledon will feature greatly later in this story.

Steady progress was made at Hillcross school, passing my eleven plus. Sad to say goodbye to Miss Field, she was not only a brilliant teacher but a great human being too.

1969. Morden Farm Middle School, set amid leafy playing fields and colourful trees in Aragon Road, Morden. The buildings were huge compared to Hillcross; there was a science block with bunsen burners, it all seemed rather intimidating to me. And this was a mixed school again, this time, the girls were taller and with more volume, shouting mainly. Add to that the bullies and puberty, a great combination. English Language was my favourite subject, the teacher Mr. McDonald being kind, gentle and calm, always smiling. Reminded me so much of my Dad. During one lesson, he commented on my work, 'You have the neatest handwriting in the class Jon. It flows onto the page.' I glanced at him and smiled, 'Thank you sir, I always try my best.' His laid-back approach made me feel at ease, and that was reflected in my work. The least favourite aspect of my two-year tenure at this school was French lessons. To be honest I could not see the point of it. My teacher was Miss Plefka of Czech origin with dark satanic eyes that followed me round the room. I did not have a clue about French verbs, was not very interested. Different genres of music I was discovering were more my thing, such as Pink Floyd and the Rolling Stones. Anyway, during a class she hovered over me and said, 'Jon Carter, what does garçon mean in French?' I thought that was rather formal. 'It means waiter, Miss Plefka,' I stuttered. 'Très bien,' she shrilled, which means very good. Happy days, that got her off my back.

Amid all that excitement I felt the need to go to the toilet. Too embarrassed to raise my hand to be excused, the inevitable accident followed and I was escorted to the lavatory, staying in there for what felt like forever. The bus journey home was awkward, and I explained to Mum through my tears that my school uniform was soiled. Dear Mother dealt with this as always, straight in the wash and me in the bath!

A few weeks later all was forgiven and I was allowed on an educational school trip to Paris. A coach picked us up and proceeded to Dover, then the ferry to Calais in France. Being a busy fishing port the area reeked of fish and nothing else, it was horrendous. Thankfully we were soon on our way to the French capital, and our accommodation. A basic hotel serving stale bread, minimal butter, hard bedsprings, staff with hygiene issues. How I yearned for a cup of tea made by my parents. Milk in first, then a teabag and boiling water, tea medium shade of brown. That was how to make it! On our first full day, the Eiffel Tower was the destination. A magnificent iron structure opened in 1889, the tower dominated the landscape. We proceeded up in the elevator to the viewing platform and were treated to a breathtaking view of Paris. Sandwiches and lemonade followed, a talk by the tour guide was given. Doubtless he stood there every day imparting his knowledge. Suddenly, one of my classmates nicked his glass of beer and we were all having a sip. Cigarettes were passed round (I had just started) it was a different world all of a sudden. The guide rumbled us so the drink was poured over the side through the steel netting, this was fixed in place to help prevent 'jumpers', apparently that was a common occurrence. When we returned to ground level there was what looked like golden glass on the pavement. This was the beer that had frozen in mid-air! Some of the girls in my class strolled past saying 'Phew', referring to my toilet incident. They loved to tease me. Though I got my own back some years later, sleeping with two of them. We all had a good laugh about it! Versailles Palace was also on the agenda, a beautiful setting with countless tapestries and paintings, fountains and flowers adorning the gardens.

I learnt a great deal in France which was the whole point of it all. On return to school there was hushed silence during the French lesson. News of our antics had reached Miss Plefka, she was not amused. Her frown was deeper than usual, and I swear steam was protruding from her ears! For the rest of my time at Morden Farm I just muddled through most of the subjects, concentrating mainly on English Language. The term ended, it was over, time to get out and about.

During the Summer recess in 1971 my Father took me to one side, he had something important to tell me. We sat in the back garden sipping lemonade in the cooler evening air. Dad looked at me and smiled saying, 'Jon, when you were a small child, your Mother and I adopted you as our son, we chose you as you are very special to us.' He then explained the adoption process to me. I grinned and replied, 'Thank you Dad, you and Mum are very special too, I could not have hand-picked two better parents.' My Father stood and stretched his six-foot frame, relief was abundant.

Mum joined us and we all hugged, it was a great moment, life defining. Looking back, I appreciate why my parents waited until I was 13 before telling me, I was mature enough by then to understand it all.

Holidays passed and senior school beckoned, Rutlish High School. There I was on day one wearing my crisp new uniform, hair neatly cut and suitably petrified! Setting off on that first morning, I felt an immense sense of pride that I was adopted. Special, wanted and safe. Those feelings stay with me to this day, and always will. The school was large and imposing, all boys, a quadrangle its dominant feature. Set in Watery Lane, London SW20 since 1957, previous pupils included John Major, former Prime Minister. I had no thoughts about reaching those dizzy heights!

John Innes Park was adjacent to the school, rugby pitches as far as the eye could see, where were the football goalposts? The Headmaster Mr. Coyle donned a flowing cape and wore a mortarboard on his head, adding to the eerie atmosphere. As was always the case, older established lads picked on us new boys, and during the first week there was a mass brawl. As luck would have it however, amongst the new arrivals was a huge lad called Ian, nicknamed Biffo. It soon became apparent how he acquired that title when he floored two sixth-formers with one punch. We became friends, and the bullies left us alone thereafter. Amongst my subjects was Physics which I did not understand, but I made an effort to look interested, even raising my hand giving wrong answers. Again, English was my beacon of hope. I knuckled down, all my homework was correct and on time.

The first year passed quickly and I scraped through my exams. I had taken to rugby, albeit reluctantly. The school was blessed with a top sports teacher, Pat Lavery, long hair and always wearing a tracksuit. He even referred to me as J.C. We became good friends, one of the lads! Selected for the reserve team, prop forward was my role and I knocked the opposition over just for the hell of it. There was a big rivalry with Wimbledon College, we loved kicking lumps out of them! During break times girls from a local school used to hang around nearby. One of them, Christine, took a shine to me. She used to call out 'I love you J.C.' Pat Lavery commented, 'Looks like you have a fan club there.' I laughed, replying, 'It would appear to be that way sir!'

Disturbingly, there was a dark side to the teaching fraternity, Mr. Barnaby, the Latin teacher. I always thought he was creepy and smarmy, noticing that he often stared at one of the rugby lads in particular. It transpired he was a 'bandit', if you get my drift, and attempted to accost that boy in the showers after a match. We taught him a lesson he would never forget, administering a good kicking. He resigned soon after that episode, embarrassed and humiliated.

By the time I reached fifteen in 1973 I was drinking at a pub near the school, 'Ye Olde Leathers Bottle' was now my regular haunt. Situated in Kingston Road, London SW19, it was owned by Truman Brewery, a jazz band played on Sunday evenings. Long locks and facial hair enabled me to swing it, and a few jars were sunk with Pat the sports coach. Pat and J.C. on the lash, good times!

The final term at Rutlish was 'O' levels. The only subject I was remotely interested in was English Language, the rest were a waste of time. Maths completely fuddled my brain. What was pie r squared when it's at home? The only pie I knew about was in the canteen! During that period of time there was an interesting new recruit to the teaching staff; Janice, longhaired sweet-smelling pottery maestro. In an all-boys school? You could whiff the testosterone a mile away, there was a long queue for lessons and I was in that queue! Janice was awesome. I ran errands for her to hopefully curry favour. My hormones were all over the place, and to watch her hands shaping a lump of wet clay was something to behold. Alas, I never got close to her, not for the want of trying. Story goes that a few older lads had success, lucky bastards! The term concluded, I completed my exams and passed the one expected and hoped for. Tangible relief. End of school forever. Wish I had done better but never had the attention span. As I wandered home on that last day, I wondered how my future was going to unfold. What would be my destiny?

CHAPTER 2

Liberation

The Summer of 1974. Free from the anxiety of exams, I felt I could breathe again. Just an awesome time, not a care in the world. I hung around with friends and visited my grandmother who lived in Clapham Junction, London on the Peabody estate. A labyrinth of flats and walkways, together with a playground. She used to make sensational scones, washed down with copious amounts of tea. We sat and watched wrestling on the small black and white television and smoked cigarettes. Gran remarked one day, 'Take these fags and hide them in your sock drawer. Don't tell your mother.' Comedy moments, she was lovely.

Mum's sister Doris, my auntie, used to pop over to our house for Sunday lunch, she lived in New Malden, Surrey, about two miles from us. Her and Mum were like two peas in a pod, very close. They were both evacuated to Cornwall during the war. I also spent an enjoyable week in Derbyshire with a couple of lads from the church, exploring the walking trails of the Peak District and scaling Mam Tor, a 517 metre hike near Castleton. Whilst at the summit of that hill I began to contemplate my future. August was drawing to a close and decisions had to be made. On returning home I chatted to Dad about my options. Given that my Father was well-established with the Post Office, reaching Head of Group status, it seemed logical to try for a job within that organisation. Dad said, 'That is a great idea son, get on the first rung of the work ladder, I will make some enquiries.' I beamed and replied, 'Thanks Dad, I can always rely on you!'

Within a fortnight a letter arrived inviting me for an interview at Camelford House, a large office block located at Vauxhall, London, right beside the River Thames. Dad had worked there for many years before relocating to Moorgate, he had contacts. We were all thrilled and Mum bought me my first suit for the occasion. Looking smart and dapper I arrived for my appointment, nervous and excited in equal measure. My role was explained to me, duties included filing, photocopying, making tea, and my title was to be Clerical Assistant. That all sounded straightforward. The interview concluded and I would be notified in due course.

Watching Dad leave for work each morning I hoped I would soon be joining him. Nervously waited for the postman, nothing in the first week. Then a letter dropped on the doormat. I could not open it quick enough. Success! A job offer was enclosed to start the following week, and we had a huge lunch to celebrate.

On that first Monday morning Mum smiled and gave me a cheery wave. 'Good luck son,' she said, looking a picture in her smart slacks and cream top. I walked up Woodland Way with Dad to catch the train at our local station, South Merton. I had walked past that landmark many times en route to Rutlish, now I was in a different environment. Change at Wimbledon, then on to Vauxhall. Before I disembarked Dad smiled said, 'All the best Jon, have a great day, I am very proud of you.' 'Thank you Dad,' I stuttered, my nerves jangling by this point. I stood on the platform as Dad proceeded to Waterloo where he caught the Tube to Moorgate.

On arrival at Camelford House I was greeted by the doorman who directed me to my office. Taking a deep breath I walked in and met my supervisor Elsie, a grand middle-aged lady. She put me at ease and showed me around, introducing me to all the staff for whom I would carry out clerical duties. Elsie chain-smoked, much to the consternation of some but I did not mind. 'Come with me, I will show you the filing system. And you could do with a haircut,' she laughed. I smiled and replied, 'Maybe one day!' The view from the office window was breathtaking, the vast expanse of London stretched into the distance. To my right sat Westminster Bridge, and clearly in view were the Houses of Parliament and of course the Abbey, scene of my greatest triumph as a choirboy. My mind wandered back to that day, it all felt rather surreal.

During the 1970s the capital lived under the threat of terrorism, there was an air of trepidation. However, live life as normal was the mantra, never give in to those thugs. Always stay vigilant. I settled into my job meeting interesting people and stunning ladies in various departments. The canteen was the pivotal area to chat them up. My confidence was growing, and as I was earning £57 pounds a week I gave Mum a tenner for housekeeping. She was so happy! A fiver stretched all evening at the 'Olde Leather Bottle', I felt like a millionaire.

Drinking in there one night after work I met Janet. Blonde, well-formed and from a traveller's background. She was sat alone. I kept glancing over trying to muster up the courage to make a move.

Eventually, Janet approached the bar to replenish her drink and we got chatting. 'Nice to meet you,' I whispered, 'not seen you here before.' Not exactly original but it was all I could think of. 'Likewise,' she replied, 'let's sit down.' Before long we were talking and laughing, downing a few drinks. Janet was fun! I felt comfortable with her. The evening passed in a blur and I offered to walk her home which was accepted. This went better than I had hoped, I stayed the night and lost my virginity to her. It transpired she was a sex addict and supported Manchester United. We all have our cross to bear I suppose. Trying to convince Janet that

Wimbledon Football Club were superior proved to be a difficult task, she laughed mockingly. Many years later we beat her team, and more than once!

Her mother made us breakfast in bed, it seemed the norm in that household. Don't think they were the church-going types. Janet owned one pop single by 'Typically Tropical', the title being 'Oh, we're going to Barbados.' Before long I knew the words backwards and in ten different languages. One Saturday I took her to watch Wimbledon, she wore her United scarf, we were playing Bognor Regis Town! Back then there were single carriages on trains, so on the way to the game we had sex. It was non-stop at every opportunity, she wanted it all the time. We went out for a few months, by then she was getting rather clingy so I called it a day. Janet protested saying she was pregnant. This turned out to be false as she had padding beneath her blouse. We went our separate ways. Some twenty years later I bumped into her, she had six children. Reckon I dodged a bullet there!

The following year some momentous events unfolded, kicking off with my beloved non-league Wimbledon drawn away to First Division Burnley in the F.A. Cup third round. And we won one-nil. A seismic shock in the football world. Who would we play in the next round? All ears were tuned to the radio for the draw on the following Monday morning. Leeds United away. Never, no way, impossible. The next home league game was crazy, the queue for tickets snaked into the distance.

On a freezing January morning I was amongst six hundred and eighty intrepid souls setting off from Wimbledon station towards Yorkshire for our date with destiny. A plentiful supply of alcohol and pies were on offer. I could not believe we were about to play Leeds with all their international players on show. Bremner, Charlton, and Lorimer; all household names. Let battle commence.

As the train approached Leeds Central station vast industrial units dominated the landscape; a grey winter's day added to the apprehension I was feeling. Far from the safety of home, I was beginning to think the trip was a bad idea. Anyway, we were there, too late to change my mind. There were huge crowds making their way to the stadium, pushing and shoving, shouting and swearing. The arena was huge compared to ours. Just prior to kick-off four blokes dressed as Wombles (our nickname) ran onto the pitch dancing and waving. They were promptly pelted with missiles by hooligans and disappeared back down the tunnel at a rate of knots. I was concerned this might turn ugly.

The teams appeared, what drama would unfold? I sensed another upset. The game began and Leeds kept the ball well, we were chasing shadows. After all, they had been English champions and knew their stuff. Chances came and went, we stayed resolute. Half-time arrived, the match still level. I turned to my friend Steve and said, 'So far so good mate, we are still in the game.' Steve nodded and gave a gloved thumbs up, it was very cold.

On resumption they increased the tempo. A rasping shot from Lorimer stung the hands of Dickie Guy, our goalkeeper, soon to become a legend in Wimbledon folklore. We then had a rare chance, Ian Cooke our captain, just failed to connect with a header. Two minutes to play and a replay at Plough Lane beckoned. That would be dreamland! Then, their winger danced into the penalty area, our full-back Bob Stockley went for a tackle and just mis-timed it. Penalty to Leeds. The home crowd roared, surely we could not lose in this way after all the effort the team had put in. The penalty area was cleared by the referee. Lorimer placed the ball on the spot and stepped back. Dickie Guy, resplendent in all-green kit, waited on his line. It was a clean strike, but the legend dived to his right and pushed the ball away. Stockley smashed it into row 'Z' and a draw was achieved. We were going crazy, but were then ambushed by a mob of angry Leeds fans. I have never understood that mentality. We scattered and made our way to the station, no police in sight. Three of our fans were stabbed, and another was shot in the testicles with an air rifle. He went on to lose one, the poor sod. By the time we boarded the train, we were pretty shaken up.

Then the police appeared, where were they earlier? They told us to lay on the floor and keep away from the windows, because the lunatics were on the bridge armed with bricks and paving slabs. As our train departed, there was a shocking series of thuds as the masonry smashed onto the roof. It was very scary. On arrival at Wimbledon, I was aghast at the condition of our train; five windows out, huge dents in the roof. Some fans went to the pub to reflect on the day.

The replay was scheduled for the following Tuesday at Plough Lane. Heavy rain ensued all day, and then came the dreadful news: Postponed, water-logged pitch. The game was played the following week at Selhurst Park, home of Crystal Palace.

The demand for tickets was huge; fans from virtually every London club turned up to support us. There was a mutual dislike for Leeds United. They brought five hundred supporters and they were battered. I don't condone that behaviour, but it was pay-back for what happened. We had more chances than during the first match, but in the end lost to a deflected goal and we were out of the F.A. Cup. I was in tears at the end, so cruel to lose in that fashion. To this day, some fifty years later, I still feel a sense of injustice. But that is life. One consolation, Leeds lost to Derby in the next round. On returning to work, my colleagues consoled me but I was quiet all day. On the journey home that evening I reflected on what might have been.

A few weeks later I was plodding through the day as usual, carrying out my normal duties. It was a relaxed atmosphere and Elsie was addressing me as J.C., the word had spread! Then all of a sudden I began to feel unwell, I had a stomach ache and fever. It was time to clock off by then, so I made my way out of the building and onto Vauxhall bridge. I was feeling really rough and collapsed onto the pavement, sweating and feeling sick. A lady appeared and said, 'My name is Laura, I'm a district nurse. Don't panic, I will go and get help.' She placed her jacket beneath my head and ran to a nearby phone box to raise the alarm. No mobiles back in those days. Laura returned and an ambulance soon arrived. 'Thank you,' I gasped, almost unconscious by that point. I had no recollection of anything thereafter until I awoke in St. Helier Hospital in Sutton the following day. Feeling rather groggy I slowly opened my eyes and there were Mum and Dad at my bedside. My ever-reliable parents. Also present was a doctor who explained that my appendix had been close to bursting, and I was operated on the previous evening. I drank some water and then dropped off to sleep for what felt like forever. When I awoke, there was a visitor for me, Laura the District nurse had kept track of my progress, like my guardian angel. Although very weak I mustered up a few words, 'Thank you so much for looking after me and keeping me safe,' I said. 'You are very welcome Jon, I was just doing my job,' she replied. That attitude is so typical of our wonderful medical professionals, always there when needed. I began to slowly recover and was allowed home, only for the wound to become infected, so two weeks off work turned into six. A nurse visited once a week to change the dressing, and I went for many walks with Mum to Morden Park, gradually regaining my strength. I recall thinking how fortunes can change in an instant.

Eventually, life resumed as normal, I returned to work back in the old routine. Everyone was pleased to see me. Elsie bought me a cake, How sweet! Having just turned seventeen, I began driving lessons every Saturday morning. My instructor Reggie smoked like a trouper, I could barely see the windscreen! He said, 'Just whack it in first gear and keep the clutch down Jon.' They were his methods of teaching, Unconventional, but it worked, I took ten lessons and passed my test first time.

When I broke the great news to my parents, they were overjoyed. Given the ordeal I had recently been through it was a big achievement. While we were having supper they informed me that a family holiday to Yugoslavia had been booked, departing a fortnight later. I was so excited, having never flown before. The two-week break tied in with my annual leave, another absence from work, this time in a good way!

Departure day was upon us, and Dad drove to Gatwick airport, a crazy place, so busy. We checked in and before long, were up and away. I felt fine on the plane, taking it all in and enjoying refreshments. Back then, smoking was permitted, I indulged as did Dad, puffing away on his pipe. We duly arrived at Dubrovnik, the extreme heat being apparent. On locating our tour guide, we were heading for our first destination, a seventy mile journey to Orebić. This attractive port town located on the Dalmatian Coast is directly across a strait from the town of Korčula, located on the island of the same name. On arrival, we freshened up and enjoyed dinner, then early nights all round, it had been a long day. The week was fun, sunbathing on a stunning sandy beach - topless women everywhere, my hormones were in overdrive. Activities included crazy golf, table tennis and badminton, not to mention monopoly and scrabble. One excursion took us to Villa Korta Katarina and Winery, we brought back some samples of course! We also visited the monastery of Our Lady of Andela, stunning architecture indeed. Before long, luggage was being packed and we were heading for Dubrovnik for the second leg of our holiday.

On boarding our transport a different tour representative loomed into view, Long brown hair, blue eyes, slim and elegant. I took one look at her and fell in love. We set off and she introduced herself as Tamara, giving the usual chat about the area and our destination. Mum commented, 'You have stars in your eyes Jon, I know that look.' My Mother never missed a trick.

After a few miles negotiating steep hill passes and winding bends, there was a calm atmosphere, people chatting and laughing, taking photographs. All looking forward with anticipation to the Dubrovnik Palace Hotel. All of a sudden, as another sharp bend was being negotiated, the driver began shouting and furiously pumping the brake pedal. This caused alarm and panic amongst us all. Mercifully, we made it onto a gentle downward slope and ground to a halt with the driver slumped over the steering wheel. What heroics from him. The brakes had failed, it had been a close shave. Fortune smiled upon all of us. As luck would have it we were about a mile from a small village and Tamara escorted us there. On arrival, bread and sardines were the order of the day, together with wine or water.

A few hours later, the coach appeared, fully topped up with brake fluid, and we continued our journey.

As the name implies, our hotel was plush with deep-pile carpets and gold-plated taps! American guests puffing on large cigars adorned the bar area, menus were stunning as was the waitress! A varied choice of activities and excursions were available to choose from, one in particular to Mostar with the famous bridge stood out. Tamara gave a talk about its history, the bridge being a medieval reconstruction marvel of architecture standing two hundred feet in height. All fascinating stuff, and beautiful, but none of it could hold a candle to her.

My parents and I stood on the bridge and took photographs, an experience never to be forgotten. 'I am so glad we are here, what a wonderful place,' Dad commented, 'Thank goodness we are all safe'. I concurred with that statement and turned to Mum and Dad, saying, 'Thank you, this is the best holiday ever'. They looked really happy, that pleased me greatly as I was becoming very protective towards them, there was a special bond between us. Tamara glanced over so I plucked up the courage to speak to her. 'Hi, I'm Jon, thank you for the tour today and you look very smart.' I felt my face was turning scarlet and butterflies were jumping in my stomach! She smiled and said, 'Thank you Jon, my name is Tamara. I am pleased you all had a good day.' Of course, I already knew her name from the talks she had given, and the badge on her uniform, but the least it broke the ice.

The following day we went to a fish picnic on the beach where locally caught fresh sardines were cooked and much wine consumed. My Dad, not being used to copious amounts of alcohol, did a 'Charlie Chuckle' and parted company with his false teeth. Following much scrambling about in the surf they were located and returned to their rightful owner! The week had passed too quickly, I had to see Tamara and found her in the coffee bar. She looked up and I held her hand tightly, gazing into her blue eyes. Went for it and kissed her, and I mean kissed! 'I'm going home today, any chance we can meet again?', I stuttered. Tamara was shedding a tear, 'I'm afraid not Jon, my job would always be a hindrance,' she replied, 'But rest assured I will always remember you.' We hugged each other and said our goodbyes. So that was that, I was gutted. I forlornly trudged to the hotel to assist with the luggage. We boarded the coach to the airport and were sorry to leave Dubrovnik with its huge stone walls constructed in the 16th century, a magnificent place.

As our plane took off, I thought of Tamara and would never forget her.

On returning home it felt like a damp squib after such a great time, back to mundane matters like work. On a positive note my beloved team Wimbledon won the Southern League title, the first of what would be three in a row. Great stuff, I got a buzz each time I watched them. Back at the pub, no sign of Janet; She was engaged and pregnant by then, lads were in and out of her like a fiddler's elbow. Nice girl, but not many scruples! Some friends and I booked tickets to see Elton John at Wembley Stadium, a twelve hour extravaganza that included The Beach Boys and The Eagles.

As Elton belted out 'I'm still standing', it felt rather apt as I reflected on the year that was nearly passed.

It had been both exciting and turbulent, opposite ends of the spectrum, so to speak. This was a learning curve, teaching me the realities of life and how to deal with different situations as they came along. It was good grounding for what lay ahead on my pathway through some very difficult times.

CHAPTER 3

Transformation

By 1976 I had reached the milestone age of eighteen; Adulthood. By law, drinking in a pub was now legal though I had been indulging in that pleasure already. It felt great to be a man and my parents gifted me a silver beer tankard with my name and age inscribed. To celebrate the occasion we enjoyed a sumptuous meal that evening prepared by Mum. I recalled days of my childhood when I was at school, together with observing Dad carrying out various tasks in our home, one of which was decorating. He was continuously sanding down the same doorframe, and on enquiring why, he said, 'Jon, this is all about the preparation. If you fail to prepare then prepare to fail.' Those wise words have always guided me. Being a Wimbledon fanatic, I began a small weekly investment in the football pools. A coupon collector called each week and I dreamt of hitting the jackpot. Mum's sense of humour came to the fore, she laughed and commented, 'There is more chance of you flying to the moon than winning the pools. The odds against success are huge!' Feeling crestfallen, I grinned and said, 'Well, I may as well try, it is too cold on the moon anyway!' We both laughed heartily. And of course Mum was correct as always. I never won a carrot.

Located between our road and Hillcross Avenue in Morden was Central Ward Residents Club, serving the community of the surrounding area, particularly the Central Ward. The land was originally part of a golf course and the club was established in 1939. Having viewed the comings and goings from my bedroom window, I was now old enough to join as a paid-up member.

At the rear of the premises sat a large field where I played as a child with my friends, now the club was another watering hole! After completing my application I was presented with a membership card, many drinking sessions were to take place! The following weekend I paid my first visit and was struck by the genial atmosphere, laughter emanating from the patrons. Once seated with a pint I soon got chatting, feeling relaxed and confident.

A nice chap introduced himself as Roy Clayton, he worked in Fleet Street for the Daily Mirror as a typesetter. And furthermore he followed Wimbledon Football Club so we soon bonded as friends. His best mate was Reg Brice, they always sat together. Both were in their late thirties and made me feel welcome. Meanwhile at work, promotion to Clerical Officer soon followed and I was relocated to Blackfriars Road, in London SE1.

My journey was slightly altered, one further stop to Waterloo then a short walk to my office. The main duties I was tasked with were dealing with Post Office contracts, better than making tea, someone else did that for me! I soon settled into my interesting new role. At Waterloo station I noticed a flower seller who had a stall just near the entrance. He was a cheery soul and I soon discovered his identity as Buster Edwards, infamous for his role in the Great Train Robbery in 1963. Having served his time in prison, Mr. Edwards, as I always greeted him, was just trying to scratch a living, fair play to him for that.

My boss Lynn was pleased with my progress and we went for the odd drink now and again at lunchtimes. She was forever going on about her husband's dodgy back so I sensed an opportunity, and took her for a meal after work.

We had a pleasant evening but sadly it was not going any further. Lynn had too much to lose. Never mind, can't win them all. Dad and I went to watch Crystal Palace play Birmingham at Selhurst Park, the home teams' stadium. Back then, one end of the ground was just a large hill so we basked in the sunshine as the match unfolded. I glanced across to see Dad was asleep, his pipe still in his mouth. 'Wake up Dad, it's half-time, how about a cup of tea,' My Father blinked in the sunlight and said, 'All that excitement made me doze off, this lot couldn't score if they played until midnight!.' This turned out to be a correct prediction, as the game ended in a goalless stalemate. We chose that game as those two sides were amongst my collection of Subbuteo teams, the concept being to flick tiny figures of footballers at a ball into the goalposts. We played this on Sundays at home when I was a child, using a green baize cloth as a pitch. Mum was not too impressed when she needed to access the bathroom! That was a great day with my Father, spending quality time together.

A few years passed and I was beginning to get bored with my job. Same old routine, faceless suits on the train. Was this it for the rest of my working life? I just felt hemmed in and trapped, grateful though I was to be employed. Time for a change of direction. On visiting the club that evening I chatted to Roy about my dilemma. His response was remarkably candid; 'You must follow your instincts Jon and back up your judgement. If you feel unsettled then do something about it,' he said. That seemed sound advice, in tandem with what I was thinking. 'Thanks Roy, let's have another pint!' I replied.

The following day I wrote a resignation letter giving one month's notice, and handed it to Lynn. Her jaw nearly hit the floor but she understood my reasoning. My final day at work soon arrived, I bade farewell to everyone and sauntered down to Waterloo station. On seeing Mr. Edwards, we shook hands and wished each other well. He said, 'Good luck and follow your dreams.' On the train home I wondered what the hell I had done, but there was no going back now. The tricky part was explaining to my parents, they were surprised to put it mildly. No need to worry, they supported me as always. I went for a drink and pondered where to begin on the Monday morning that was fast approaching.

Naively, I had assumed it would be a piece of cake just to walk into another job. That was poor judgement on my part. For a change of tack I trailed around London asking at building sites for labouring work, and was met with scorn and laughter. Even the pleasure boat at Westminster Pier had no staff vacancies, I was enquiring everywhere all to no avail. At least I had money saved so no reason to panic, and on reflection decided to allow myself some space and visit a few landmarks in the City. Somewhere peaceful was preferable, so I selected the Tate Gallery located in Millbank, access to which was by Tube to Southwark. The gallery holds the nations' collection of modern art from 1900 to the present day. I marveled at the exquisite pieces on show. Next was a boat trip to Tower Bridge enabling me to enjoy the panoramic views from the Tower of London to St. Paul's Cathedral in the west and Shooters Hill to the east. The bridge took eight years to construct, opening in 1892.

What struck me was how much busier London had become, even during the four years I had been working there. More traffic and people, not to mention the pollution. It hung in the air, I could almost touch it.

A few days later I treated myself to a show at Wimbledon Theatre starring Morecambe and Wise, my all-time comedy heroes. Seated in the front row of the circle I laughed until my sides ached, tears of joy cascading down my face. During their encore, Eric looked along the line of seats and it felt like he had picked me out. Of course that was just the moment our eyes met! I will always adore Eric and Ernie, God bless them both. The laughter and applause were the reason they performed for people like me. Having spent some time just chilling out I felt better in general. It was now full steam ahead to find some work.

Whilst out for a walk I popped into my local shop for a newspaper, and on flicking through it my attention was drawn to an interesting advertisement: A betting company was crying out for Trainee Managers, no experience needed. This was an opportunity, so I called the number and was invited for an interview.

As I engaged well with people and enjoyed sport this might be the solution. It was explained to me that if I knew basic arithmetic and could think on my feet, then progress could be quite rapid with those useful attributes. My attention span was good having learnt that skill as a choirboy, excellent grounding at a young age. Once on the training course it was clear that other people had reached a crossroads in their working lives, and were trying something new.

The school ran for six weeks and I was taught how to settle bets, which to the uninitiated means working out the winnings for customers. I grasped the concept of this quickly, passed the course, and my title was Trainee Manager. I was delighted and broke the good news to my parents. They both had relief and joy etched on their faces. Mum said, 'Well done Jon, we knew you would find another job, you are resilient and determined.' 'Thanks Mum,' I replied, 'I have learnt those traits from you and Dad. You both displayed as much when you adopted me.' Big hugs all round.

I was allocated to a shop, Mecca Bookmakers near Morden. On arrival, Paul the Manager introduced himself and showed me the ropes relating to running a betting shop. His dog Basil the Basset hound was ever-present at his side. My initial task was to write the racing results on a large board, and alter the prices when they were announced over the tannoy speaker, I soon realized that when the outcome went against the customers they did not react too well! A few missiles were aimed in my direction — food mainly. Somewhat harsh as I didn't ride the horses! Paul laughed and said, 'Don't worry Jon, they are harmless, you will get used to it. The punters are our bread and butter, so just smile.' This job was different, no doubt about that. I took it all in my stride and got to know Joan and Eileen, the two cashiers, together with an elderly gentleman named Ron, a long-time friend of Paul. Ron just pottered about making tea, quite often he was asleep! One busy Saturday we were about to open the shop when Basil did his business right next to the door.

Chaos ensued, punters were banging on the door wanting to get in, and poor old Paul had to clear up the mess. Priceless. I was trained very well and took to it like a duck to water. By the age of twenty-one I was established in my own right, running different shops as a Relief Manager when required. I was comfortable in my role, but little did I realise I would soon meet somebody who would turn my life upside down.

CHAPTER 4
A New Decade

Time waits for no man, and the Seventies had flown by. Still signing cheques with 1979, I expect many people were making that error. Soon adjusted and got used to it. Margaret Thatcher was Prime Minister, encouraging us all to buy our own homes and work hard, her steely persona to the fore. A Royal marriage gripped the nation, Prince Charles had managed to bag Lady Diana Spencer, never understood why she didn't choose me, we could have gone for a drink and kebab afterwards. It's good to dream!

She probably would have enjoyed that more, to be honest. I often visited my social club to unwind, chatting to Roy and Reg. The latter was a self-employed gardener and a keen horse racing fan. The three of us took a trip to Sandown Park, located in the leafy Surrey Suburbs of Esher. The racecourse first opened in 1875. We enjoyed a fun day out with plenty of liquid refreshment, rather like a busman's holiday for me! Reg won a nice few quid and said; 'Drinks are on me tonight Lads, and the pork scratchings.' Generous to a fault. Roy laughed, saying; 'Makes a change, you are usually in the loo when it's your round!' There were two snooker tables at the club, I was intrigued so began to learn the game, meeting some interesting characters along the way. Bill Cooke, whose wife Maude worked behind the bar was an ever-present on a Sunday evening. We struck up a great friendship and played many frames together. Grasping the rudiments of the game I graduated to the match table, where all the serious stuff took place.

This was intimidating to begin with, feeling out of my depth mixing it with established players. Basic errors were prevalent but I ploughed on anyway. Standing at the bar I got chatting to Norman Edwards, a smartly dressed club stalwart with slick black hair and shirtsleeves rolled up to his elbows. He played a steady game and was never in a rush. I began to copy his style, imitation is the best form of flattery. We played many frames, often late into the night, and one evening he said, 'Jon, you are the most improved player I have seen for a long time, potting them off the lampshades!' In layman's terms this meant that any ball I hit went in the pocket. I replied, 'Thanks Norman, I am learning from the master.' Acquaintances were also made with John Lilburn and Peter Stewart, the three of us eventually forming a team to play in the Epsom and District Snooker League. More on that later.

Then one evening, there was a new face behind the bar. Short brown hair and wearing a smart suit, no one as stylish had worked there before. The Committee were all blazers and ties, so she was a breath of fresh air and a welcome addition. I bought a pint but got no eye contact, she looked a little nervous. This lady had caught my attention and was in my thoughts the following day. On my next visit she was there again. This time squeezed into blue jeans revealing a figure to die for. On obtaining some refreshment I enquired as to whether she would like a drink. A polite 'no thanks' was the response as I noticed her stunning green eyes. At least she had looked in my direction. Then the club steward called her over to talk about stocking the bar and all was revealed. Her name was Penny so I now had useful information to use.

As time went on I struck up a brief conversation. It was tricky, given how busy she was, but I made a breakthrough. 'Hi Penny, my name is Jon, large vodka and coke with ice please, and one for yourself,' was my opening gambit. Placing my drink on the bar she smiled and replied; 'Many thanks, I'll have an orange juice.' My heart was pounding out of my chest as I gave her a wink and returned to my seat, not being able to take my eyes off her as she served customers. Now and again Penny glanced over and my mind was grappling with different equations as to when to ask her out. I didn't want to put her on the spot, so gently does it was sensible. If I bided my time the chance would present itself. Meanwhile, at work I was distracted, not to the point where it affected my ability, but I kept seeing Penny in my mind's eye. I was quieter than usual and my shop clients tapped into this. One, an elderly gentleman named Derek enquired; 'You alright Jon, not your usual bouncy self today.' 'Just a migraine coming on, thanks for asking,' I replied. I hadn't shaved for three days either, better get my act together.

After work I did food shopping, just to buy basics, not feeling motivated. Wandered the aisles picking up milk, cereal, and a quiche for supper. Heading for the exit into Tooting Broadway the volume of noise from traffic was extreme. I had two days in Tooting, located in the London Borough of Wandsworth, as a relief manager. Let's just say it was not the most welcoming place to be working. Walking in the hot sunshine past a burger bar I just happened to glance to my right, and there was sat Penny, staring into space.

I seized my chance and went and sat next to her, saying; 'Hi, how are you, do you recognise me, I'm Jon from the social club.' She replied, 'How nice to see you, what are you doing around here?' We had a coffee and I explained about my job, it transpired that she lived in the Tooting area. During our conversation Penny revealed she was married but separated, her husband had conducted many affairs with other women and was a bit handy with his fists, so she had taken the bar job with a view to easing the pain. On pointing out that I lived a stone's throw from the club, she beamed and said, 'You don't have far to stagger home then, and I've spotted you in the snooker room, are you any good?' I laughed and replied; 'Not too bad, and improving. I'll teach you one day if you like!' Now the words were flowing and nerves not jangling, this was the perfect moment to propose a date. We arranged to meet in the club car park after her next shift.

A few days later that evening arrived. Whilst sat with Roy and Reg putting the world to rights, Penny was working the bar on a busy Saturday night. Admiring glances were exchanged between us, and she looked stunning in jeans and a cream blouse. The car park was at the rear of the premises so I duly made my way there, waiting for what felt like forever. Penny had to wash glasses and tables, I got through a few fags before she finally appeared, opening the doors of her blue Ford Mondeo and beckoning me into her car. She said, 'Let's park in your road away from prying eyes, don't want the rumour mill starting.' So off we went, finding a space at the far end of Woodland Way. She lit a cigarette and inhaled deeply, relief etched on her face. Chatting and laughing for several hours it felt like we had known each other for years, and we sealed the evening with a passionate kiss. That fair took my breath away. Another meeting was put in the diary before she had to drive home. I waved goodbye and went indoors feeling completely smitten. The circumstances did not put me off, quite the contrary, there was a risky edge to it that I thrived on.

May 19th, 1980, my birthday. Grand old age of twenty-two had been reached, hair was receding but still looked handsome as ever! I treated my parents to lunch at The Leather Bottle pub and we ate a hearty meal of fish and chips, topped off with sticky toffee pudding and hot cups of tea. Mum always said that tea was the best drink of the day, how right she was. Dad and I enjoyed a cigar together as was the tradition on special occasions, and we chatted about life in general. My Father knew me better than anyone and could sense a change in my demeanour. He said, 'Are you alright Jon, you seem a little distracted, your Mother and I will always listen and help if anything is worrying you.' I gave Dad a wistful smile and replied, 'I have met a new special lady, her name is Penny. She is a bit older than me, thirty-six actually, and separated from her husband.' That was a lot for Dad to take in. However, as always he was calmness personified and said, 'Well, that's nice, perhaps we can meet her, why don't you invite her round one evening.' 'Thanks Dad. I'll let her know,' was my reaction. I was thrilled with that. The next time I saw Penny the invitation was accepted. The next Friday she knocked on our front door to be greeted by my Mother, who had a live and let live approach to life, neither her or Dad were judgmental. Penny had one hour before her shift began so we all sat in the back garden talking. This broke the ice nicely. Later on, I popped in for a pint. She had a beaming smile on her face, it pleased me to see her happy. In hushed tones, she said, 'Your parents are so sweet and kind, they made me feel completely at ease, I can see where you get your good manners from.' How lovely. The foundations for our relationship were in place.

Some months passed and we were in full swing, having sex in hotels and even at my home on the odd occasion. By this time I was completely hypnotised, like a rabbit in the headlights; I viewed Penny as my girlfriend, even buying her a ring made of soft gold. We made love to the music of ABBA, her favourite band, 'Super Trouper', very endearing. Back at the club some people had cottoned on, especially the Bar Steward who was keeping a beady eye on me. He was only jealous, a portly old man who Penny wouldn't look twice at. We just played the game, no-one saw what went on away from that place!

My job had become routine and enjoyable, being able to engage with people from all walks of life was a bonus. Mum and Dad were happy that I seemed settled. From my point of view I was living the dream with the woman I loved. Then one day, Penny dropped a bombshell. Suggesting that I go to her place one evening. Bearing in mind this was her marital home I felt somewhat wary, but I agreed to anyway. I thought the world of her and would do anything, as far as I was concerned she walked on water.

On a chilly evening in early December, I caught the Tube from Morden station through to Tooting Broadway. On arrival it was pouring with rain as I sheltered in the station entrance to have a smoke. The area had a different atmosphere to that day when I met Penny in the burger bar. Feeling uncomfortable, off I headed to her house, the bright streetlamps highlighting the awful weather. I rang the doorbell and she quickly ushered me into the lounge. We chatted over a coffee. There was something different about her. I could sense it. My jeans were soon round my ankles as she got down to business. All of a sudden there was a noise outside, and Penny leapt up to peer through the net curtain. 'Oh my God, it's my husband,' she yelled, 'You will have to use the backdoor.' I heeded that advice and sprinted down the garden like a scalded cat, only to be confronted by a large coalbunker. We had one at home, I used to help Dad fill the coalbucket but this was a different scenario. I clambered over it, my hands freezing and scratched, landing the other side in a large puddle next to a long fence adorned with brambles. As I came to my senses, a deafening roar seemed to course straight through my body, the main train line was but a few yards away. Once on my feet I staggered down the alleyway adjacent to her house to check the lay of the land. There was no-one outside so it was now or never. Turning my jacket collar up against the elements, I walked as briskly as possible without looking back and made it to the station.

Eventually a train pulled in and off I set back to Morden, attracting several glances due to being covered in dirt and muck. I didn't care about that, I was glad to be alive. Penny never returned to the club and I heard on the grapevine that she was in St. George's Hospital, Tooting.

Obviously concerned, I went up there to discover she was suffering from yellow jaundice and isolated in her own room. Armed with a bunch of flowers I opened the door, she took one look at me and cried her eyes out. 'I am so sorry Jon,' she blubbed. 'Thank goodness you are in one piece.' This really hurt me to see the love of my life so upset. 'There is nothing to be sorry about, none of this is your fault,' I replied. I gently held her hand, and just to darken the mood news was broadcast on the radio in her room that John Lennon had been murdered in New York. We sat in stunned silence on hearing that. A great musician cut down in his prime by the Devil himself, a lunatic who should never have been walking the streets. Yet again, the system failed. At that point, the estranged husband Vince entered the room. This was the coward who had beaten Penny many times. I had nothing but loathing for him. He looked at me and said, 'Who are you then mate?' Thinking quickly on my feet I replied, 'I'm here representing the club, we thought some flowers would cheer Penny up.' He didn't say anything, shaking my hand instead. Wishing Penny a speedy recovery, now was my cue to vacate the premises. Walking down the corridor breathing heavily, my relief was tangible. Imagine if that mug knew what his wife had been getting up to, she had been living her life, no thanks to him. To this day I wonder how I ever got away with it.

Some weeks passed, it was a constant worry as to how Penny was doing, I had no way of contacting her. A return visit to her house was a non-starter. Sitting having a drink was difficult, I just kept staring at the bar where I first talked to her, and gazed into those gorgeous green eyes. Then one evening, when I was watching a programme with my parents, Penny turned up at our house.

We hugged in the hallway, she looked much healthier than when I last saw her. With all of us assembled in the lounge, Penny nervously cleared her throat and spoke to Mum and Dad, 'I'm very sorry but due to family circumstances, I won't be here anymore. Thank you for being so kind to me,' she said. My heart sunk, I knew this was the end. I walked Penny to her car and we kissed for the final time. She said, 'Goodbye Jon, please take care of yourself.' My eyes were streaming with tears as I watched the taillights of her vehicle disappear up Woodland Way. Headed to my room and was inconsolable. At least she had the good grace to come over. That must have been hard to do. I didn't leave my home for two days, citing having a cold to be excused from work. Mum and Dad were supportive as ever and I slowly began to realise that there was never going to be a future for Penny and I, it was just that, fantasy. I had been living in a bubble and out of touch with reality. During the following few years life eventually got back to some sort of normality which I was grateful for, after that emotional rollercoaster. However, on the horizon was an upheaval of a different nature.

CHAPTER 5

Independence

A time of seismic change; My dear Father had been offered, and accepted, early retirement from his role within The Post Office, having achieved Head of Group status in the Traffic Division. The company name later changed to British Telecom. Dad began as a postboy and worked his way up the ladder, now he had earnt the right to call it a day, age fifty-seven. Mum and I were so proud of him, through all that hard graft he had given us both a stable home environment and peace of mind. My parents were married on the 25th March 1950 at St. Stephen's Church, Battersea, and had recently celebrated their thirty-fourth anniversary. They were a wonderful example of being true to wedding vows, like two peas in a pod; inseparable. We were in the lounge, Mum enjoying a glass of sherry and Dad puffing contently on his pipe, legs crossed in his favourite armchair. Relaxed at last, no trains to rush for, just taking it easy. He had always done his research before making any decisions, and resting his pipe on the ashtray, he said; 'Jon, your Mother and I have been contemplating moving home for some time now, and we believe the time is right to do so. We have found a suitable property in Chichester, West Sussex.' I looked aghast, my job and friends were in London and I didn't want to move away. Mum noted my anxiety, saying, 'Don't worry son, we have found you a bedsit flat in the local area, and paid the deposit. The plan is to move in two weeks' time.' Thanking my parents, I replied, 'It's all rather sudden but I respect your reasoning.' So, on April 15th, 1984, there were tearful hugs as my parents set off for a new life.

My move took place the following day, which meant a night alone on an airbed laying on bare floorboards. The atmosphere was eerie and quiet. All the family history that had taken place in that house raced through my mind; my adoption, schooldays, the church choir, Westminster Abbey, holidays, and of course, Penny. I cried many tears that night.

Morning broke, I ran to a phone box and called the number my parents had given me, to my relief they had arrived safely and were in the process of unpacking. Now it was my turn, all my worldly goods were loaded into a van to make the short journey to Raynes Park, about two miles from Morden. It was such a shame to leave Woodland Way but a new era beckoned. Raynes Park is a residential suburb, situated South-West of Wimbledon Common. After settling in, I went for a walk to clear my head, having knowledge of the area made it feel quite familiar; I couldn't get lost. The nearby railway links (no coalbunkers this time!) were useful for my job, and the bus dropped me a short hop from the club. It was an odd feeling having to fend for myself, paying bills on time, going to the laundrette, cooking food. I never took living at home with my parents for granted, far from it, but I had to accept that this was the reality. I managed to visit Mum and Dad, catching the transport from Clapham Junction direct to Chichester. The journey took just shy of two hours, as the train rumbled along I wondered what lay in store when I got there. Dad was on the platform to greet me, we had a hug and lubrication at a nearby pub, then he drove us to their new home in Cedar Drive. A three-bedroom detached property with a huge back garden that looked more like an orchard! Mum gave me a cheery greeting, out came the fruitcake and tea. We sat outside as the early Spring weather was favourable. 'What a beautiful place you have,' I enthused, 'I know you will be happy here.' Dad smiled and said, 'Thanks Jon, we made the correct choice, your Mother and

I fell in love with it the first time we viewed so that sealed the deal.' Happy laughter ensued, I was thrilled with this outcome. While Mum had a nap, Dad and I went to the local club for a few frames of snooker. Back in the early 1970s, we had a vacation on the Isle of Wight at a holiday camp. In attendance was a resident professional player in the form of Graham Miles, my Father won the camp competition and the prize was to play him, one frame only. Dad potted a red and black, Mr. Miles raised an eyebrow and duly cleared the table! Great fun, and my Father was presented with a medal for his efforts. Chichester itself is a Cathedral city, and was previously a Roman and Anglo-Saxon settlement, a major market setting from those times to the present day. The Cathedral was constructed in the 12th Century, and the city walls were built on Roman foundations. Alas, it was time to head back to London. I promised my parents with whom I had a rock-solid bond that another visit would be soon.

On my return, The Raynes Park Tavern just near the station was my next port of call. I felt like having a session, it was Sunday the next day so no work. The place was somewhat rough, plenty of staring, men with tattoos pretending to be gangsters. How sad. Nevertheless, it served its purpose and several pints of lager were consumed. I noticed there was a bird propping up the bar, and she kept looking over. Soon, she tried her luck.

'You going to buy me a drink then?', she enquired. Here we go again, I thought, another freeloader. I bought her one anyway, good to have the company. A wedding ring was in evidence though that had not stopped me before! Vanessa was her name, and before I could blink we were between the sheets. Never one to look a gift horse in the mouth, it would have been rude not to. Following sex, we lay there for a while and I brought up the subject of her marital status. On establishing she had a husband I enquired as to what he did for a living. Vanessa laughed, saying, 'He's in Wandsworth prison doing fifteen years for manslaughter.' I made my excuses and beat a hasty retreat, Sod that for a game of soldiers!

Standing on my own two feet was proving to be a challenge, takeaway meals were the staple diet, not ideal. Letters left unopened, washing piled up. I missed the routine and the company. The latter being the hardest. Mum and Dad were always contactable by phone, I called them at least three times per week, but it was just not the same. My visits to Chichester were frequent, even staying there during a week off work. That was the only place I wanted to be, with them. These feelings stemmed from my adoption and upbringing, they were both my mentors and safety net. Eventually, I became accustomed to my situation because I had to, but that process was a long one.

A few years later, in 1986, Wimbledon were promoted to the First Division beating the likes of Manchester United, I wondered if Janet had watched that match! That was an incredible achievement, rising from non-league football when I began supporting them in 1965 as a wide-eyed child with my Father.

My job continued in the same vein, being a relief Manager meant I wasn't tied to one shop, which was preferable. Liaisons with various women passed like ships in the night, relationships were off the agenda for the time being. Whilst enjoying myself I upgraded to a one-bedroom flat in Derwent Road, London SW20, again near to where I was raised as a youngster. My parents travelled up to view my new place, and were overjoyed that at last I had settled down and was more in control of my emotions. A delicious roast dinner was enjoyed by the three of us, cooked by me for a change! It was great to have more space to live in, and a washing machine, I kept on top of the chores and felt happier in general.

The following year saw my team reach the quarter-finals of the F.A. Cup, Tottenham Hotspur were the opposition at our home ground, Plough Lane. After an exciting tussle we were sadly on the wrong end of a 2-0 scoreline. Glen Hoddle, of England fame, scored an unbelievable free-kick, it was a quality strike. We were all gutted, but the best team won on the day so no complaints.

Wimbledon football club were formed in 1889 as Wimbledon Old Centrals, until their name was changed in 1905. Famous players included Billy Cotton, of Big Band fame, who wore the shirt back in 1919. In 1963 the club won the F.A. Amateur Cup at Wembley Stadium, defeating Sutton United 4-2. A giant Irish centre-forward named Eddie Reynolds, six feet tall and built like a tank, scored all four goals with headers. This feat has never been equalled, and is unlikely to be. I recalled watching Eddie play when I was a kid, towards the end of his career.

Then, after all the previous disappointments and heartache, we reached the F.A. Cup Final in 1988. As an avid fan I had always hoped my team would win a major trophy. Each year, Dad and I watched the Cup Final on television, cheering on the underdogs. Now that was Wimbledon, we were playing Liverpool with their star-studded line-up. As a club we were never awash with money, making up for that with a strong team spirit and never-say-die attitude. The Chairman, Stanley Reed, had cobbled together a squad mainly from non-league, including free transfers, a labourer and even a hod-carrier. The latter went by the name of Vinnie Jones and the team were labelled 'The Crazy Gang' by the tabloids, so-called as they got up to no end of mischief, including spraying reporters with beer, letting down the managers' car tyres, food in players' socks and so on. The Manager, Bobby Gould, accepted it and just left them to their own devices.

I spotted a few players on the lash in Wimbledon Village on the eve of the Final, that was just the way they geared up for any match! So, at 3 P.M. on Saturday 14th May, our date with destiny began. The players, resplendent in their blue kit with yellow trim, had stood proudly for the National Anthem, the weather was warm and still. Roy was with me, and I said, 'I think this is our day my friend, just got a feeling.' The game was frantic. In the early stages, Vinnie clattered into Steve McMahon leaving the Liverpool midfielder writhing in agony. This earned just a ticking off from the referee, Vinnie had left his calling card! Then, in the 37th minute, Lawrie Sanchez scored for Wimbledon with a glancing header. The second half saw Liverpool pile on the pressure, and they were awarded a very contentious penalty.

Our full-back Clive Goodyear clearly made contact with the ball first, but the spot-kick was given. The Wimbledon goalkeeper and captain, Dave Beasant, nick-named Lurch due to his long arms, sprung to his left and saved it, he had obviously watched Dickie Guy against Leeds back in 1975! Justice had been served, that was never a penalty in a million years. This was an historic moment, the first time a penalty had been saved in an F.A. Cup Final. We held firm and secured a 1–0 victory. On our return, Wimbledon town centre was going mental, all the pubs ran out of draft lager, just bottles left. On the following day the team paraded with the trophy, then on the Monday evening there was a testimonial game at Plough Lane for veteran striker Alan Cork, he had served the club so well over many seasons. Before kick-off, there on a rickety table was the F.A. Cup, shining so brightly. Little old Wimbledon, who defied the odds and achieved greatness. I felt so proud and grateful to be part of their meteoric journey.

Back at the club we talked about little else, everyone was buzzing. My standard of snooker improved after watching Alex Higgins on television. I quickened the pace and played on adrenalin like he did. Obviously, Alex was in a different universe to me as regards ability, I was fascinated by his twitching and body movement on the shot. Mimicking his voice as I walked around the table was entertaining and it gave me an edge, to the extent that I had a mindset to only win, defeat was not an option. One evening, when I was practising alone, the aforementioned John and Peter turned up for a game. We sat there over a drink, and Peter said, 'I have entered us to play for The Skinner Cup, our first round match is next week.' The Cup was so-named after a former club member, the trophy centre stage in a cabinet near the bar. This made a change from bread and butter league games, the three of us were a good team; the format was the same, two frames each to play. We cruised through the first two rounds, reaching the semi-finals to play Highfield Club Sutton, on their home table. They were tricky opponents, the match went to a deciding frame which Peter won on the black. The final was at the same venue, neutral to us and Coulsdon, our nemesis in the league. John played first followed by Peter, the frames were shared in a tight, tactical affair. There was a sandwich interval, and with the scores level it was all down to me. I had decided beforehand to play safe and wait for an opening, a game plan worked on my increasingly frustrated opponent. He had no answers. I cleared the blue, pink and black to win comfortably. Central Ward Residents Club had won the Skinner Cup! At the presentation we were given the trophy and a replica each. I still have mine to this day.

As the decade was drawing to a close it was clear to me that I had the tools to survive anything that was thrown at me. My resilient nature and mental fortitude had served me well thus far, both were going to be severely tested as future events unfolded.

CHAPTER 6
Dark Moments

In the early 1990's I met Sarah, a nurse at my local hospital. Six feet tall, auburn hair, great physique; Fitness instruction three evenings per week on top of the day job kept her very busy. We went out and about, she loved bowling, always beating me. A great cook too, Chinese dishes were second to none. Just a regular lady with no drama, someone normal for a change. Sarah and I had a mutual agreement that our relationship remained platonic, both of us having been traumatised by past experiences. Sexual activity took place now and again, but within that parameter. Quite often we went to Cinatra's, our favourite nightclub, which was located in Croydon, a large town in South London. The area had a rich history; at the beginning of the 19th Century Croydon became the terminus of two pioneering commercial transport links with London. Nowadays, it was a really rough area with a high crime rate, vigilance was the key to survival. One Friday evening we paid a visit, the venue was on two levels, dancing on the ground floor and food upstairs. It was lively and packed to the rafters; friends mingling and drinking, scantily clad ladies in cages dancing on the stage, and the disc maestro playing his set. Two defining characters who frequented the club scene were present, always together, joined at the hip, Sweaty Betty and Scary Mary, legends of clubland. Betty was a buxom woman, with numerous tattoos and arms like Popeye. Grown men used to cry into their beer when she beat them at arm wrestling, and when Betty danced, the tables vibrated and ice jumped out of glasses. Mary was a tall, lean lady who never smiled and sported facial stubble. She used to strike a match on her chin to light her pipe; Seriously, Mary smoked a pipe, not the same type Dad used but a longer, thinner version. There was much speculation as to the contents of it! They commanded the dance floor, and unsurprisingly nobody else got in their way. We ordered some drinks, lager for me and orange juice for Sarah. Being into fitness she never got drunk, just danced all night. And could she dance! A very athletic lady with muscular features on show, towering half a foot above me. Mick the manager served us, we had known him for some time, he ran a tight ship and that was reflected in the crowds that always turned up. 'Busy tonight Mick,' I said, 'The place is jumping.' Mick replied, 'Yes, it's good, but there is a firm sitting down near the stage. I'm keeping an eye on them.' I went for a wander to survey the area, and sure enough there were five men at a table drinking shots. That in itself was not unusual, it was a nightclub after all. However, Mick's instincts were usually spot-on so I made a mental note of their faces. Drawing heavily on my roll-up, I spotted Sarah cutting some serious shapes amongst the throng of people. I stood and sipped my drink, she would find me when it all calmed down a bit.

While leaning against the bar absorbing the atmosphere, I noticed a problem developing within the seated areas, food was being thrown amid the sound of breaking glass. This was typical behaviour by groups of men who could not hold their drink, while most of us just enjoyed ourselves and got on with life, there was a small minority who were not wired correctly upstairs if you get my drift. Maybe the authorities should have put them on a large raft and set it adrift, however, I doubt that notion would have been passed in Parliament! More likely to award them more benefit money to squander on drink and drugs.

The music had stopped, women were screaming, the scene was chaotic. Then, as I drew closer, it became clear that the firm Mick had highlighted earlier were indeed the perpetrators. One of them, a very overweight individual, launched himself forward straight into Sarah. He grappled and touched her inappropriately. She was attempting to get away, all to no avail. After shouting at him to leave her alone, he turned and took a swing at me. I ducked out of the way and knocked him out cold with one punch. Another wannabe gangster taken care of. His mates just stood rooted to the spot, they didn't fancy any of that! I stared at the man laying flat out on the floor, he would have got out of breath making a cup of tea.

Sarah was in shock and hugging me, 'Thanks, Jon,' she said. 'You are the essence of goodness, I always feel safe with you.' I stroked her hair, and replied, 'I've always got your back Sarah, no-one will ever hurt you on my watch.'

Paramedics duly arrived and attended to the ugly brute with the badly broken nose, the police were then buzzing about, being a nuisance. On questioning me, I pointed out that my retaliation was justified, and he deserved it. Protection of Sarah was paramount. The Sergeant enquired as to whether I had a police record, my cheeky response was that I'd got *Walking on the Moon* in my collection, and he could borrow it if he liked. He looked at me with disdain, and I would be in touch. Some people have no sense of humour!

A few days passed, Sarah was feeling a little better. The incident had been a terrifying experience, nobody had a right to assault her and she was staying at my home for the time being, until fully recovered. One morning, we were relaxing, enjoying a coffee when there was a knock on the door. The sergeant and his mate were standing on the doorstep so I invited them in. To my horror, they informed me that I was under arrest for grievous bodily harm with intent. Despite protesting my innocence, the handcuffs were applied and I was led away. Sarah was in bits; this was not going to aid her healing from that dreadful ordeal. The next day I appeared in front of the local magistrate, my legal team entered a *not guilty* plea. Bail was then refused, held in police custody was the setting as there were no prison spaces. I was relieved about that; A crumb of comfort at least. An appeal against the charge was submitted by my solicitor on the grounds that I used proportionate force to defend myself. I pointed out that if I had hit my assailant properly he never would have got up. With hindsight, that was not the wisest comment to make, and was not part of the submission. I just said that in the heat of the moment.

The day of my Crown Court trial arrived. I stood there in my best suit, Sarah was in the public gallery with her Mother. This damn process dragged on for many hours, then finally a verdict; *Not guilty*. I felt the weight lift from my shoulders, whoops of delight from the gallery. My lawyer informed that Mick had come forward as a witness, confirming I used self-defence. Understandably, he had been reluctant to begin with, fearing repercussions from the other gang members. I completely respected Mick and his reasoning. The judge bound me over to keep the peace, looking like my former headmaster, and advised me to be careful in the future.

Outside the Court I sat with Sarah, and freedom had never tasted sweeter. She was the light of my life, I had done right by her and always would.

The following Saturday Mick closed the club to the general public, with just a select crowd allowed in. There were about fifty of us reflecting on recent events, and we all enjoyed a great evening to celebrate my freedom. Many toasts to the fact that justice had prevailed. Betty & Mary's attempts at dancing caused much hilarity, they were great sports. Sarah just kept smiling at me, and likewise back. While we were never going to become seriously involved, she would always hold a special place in my heart. The lesson I learnt from this whole experience was to always protect those close to me, no matter what the circumstances, and never be bullied or show weakness. I had stepped up to right a wrong, and would do so again if ever called upon.

In the meantime, however, I yearned for a change in direction, and opportunities were soon to present themselves taking me out of my comfort zone.

CHAPTER 7

New Challenges

Same old routine each day has applied to most of us at some time or another, the fatigue that can cause was holding me back; I needed a stimulus, an incentive. Moaning about it was never going to achieve anything, so I did some digging about at my local library to try and get some inspiration.

On the notice board, there was a flyer containing information about a charity walk to raise much needed funds for the Cystic Fibrosis Trust. This venture was being organised by U.K. Outdoor Pursuits, and the venue was Ben Nevis mountain, in Scotland, the concept being to follow the hill-walkers path to the top. This company offered a variety of open-air challenges in different regions within the British Isles; activities included mountain walking, canoeing, abseiling and rock climbing to name but a few.

I enquired by phone, gathering several names who wished to support this worthy cause. Cystic Fibrosis is a debilitating genetic disorder that impairs normal clearance of mucus from the lungs and facilitates infection by bacteria, notably *staphylococcus aureus*. This terrible disease renders sufferers breathless and weak — so raising money for research into a cure was vital.

After purchasing a decent pair of walking boots, I did a few laps of Morden Park to break them in, had to harden up my feet so as to try and avoid blisters.

The date of the trip arrived, the assembly point was Brent Cross Coach Terminus in North London; there were other single travellers looking equally apprehensive, but once we all boarded the transport that feeling quickly evaporated.

The journey was a long one, roughly twelve hours. Despite regular stops for refreshments, I still managed to set off the smoke alarm in the toilet trying to sneak a fag. This earned me a warning from the coach driver, one more indiscretion and I was off, like being given a yellow card in football!

Our destination was Fort William, a town in the western Scottish Highlands. Located on the shores of Loch Linnhe, it was known as the gateway to Ben Nevis and in the town centre sat the West Highland Museum which focused on regional life and history. Ben Nevis is the highest peak in the British Isles, rising to 1345 metres. In old money that is 4,408 feet. It stood at the western end of the Grampian mountains, in the Highland region of Lochaber.

I had never seen anything like it. Mam Tor in Derbyshire was but a hillock in comparison. On arrival I got settled in, and we were all summoned to the hotel lobby for a pep talk given by Wayne Naylor, the chief instructor from Outdoor Pursuit. He was at pains to point out that although this was going to be an enjoyable adventure run by experienced mountain guides, extreme caution was needed.

The forces of nature took no prisoners, down the years walkers had fallen victim to its powers by straying from the designated route. That sound advice was taken on board, and I tucked into bed for an early night.

After a hearty breakfast I took the short walk to the pre-arranged meeting point, my rucksack bulging with essential supplies, namely water, chocolate, sandwiches and wet-proof clothing.

On Saturday 16th July 1994, my ascent began. This was what I had been searching for, a diversion from the mundane monotony of daily life.

Three guides accompanied the group, one at the front, middle and rear. They were well-versed in safety procedures,

Veterans at what they did. The weather was fair, not too hot, the trail wound its way up a gradient that was manageable for anyone with a decent level of fitness. Pausing for a water break, I took in the breathtaking view. Mountain passes as far as the eye could see, total peace and quiet save for the whistling wind. A sense of freedom washed over me, especially given the recent incarceration I had endured; tranquility was in charge.

Having captured some great images on my camera, I proceeded along the zig-zag pathways that led to 'Windy Corner', the scheduled stop for lunch and a massage to my legs. Of course, ablutions had to be taken care of; when you've got to go, you've got to go. Maybe a thousand years from now, fossil hunters may discover my hidden gem and claim it to be a piece of moon rock; stranger things have happened!

The corner lived up to its billing, a gale was blowing. After further progress, snow was encountered. Thank goodness for thick walking socks. It always snowed on 'The Ben', as the locals named it.

Finally, the summit was reached, we were allocated half an hour for photos and sustenance as the weather often closed in rapidly. Sunshine and fog within five minutes was not uncommon. A group photo displaying the Cystic Fibrosis banner was taken, along with one of me standing on the plinth, 'nowhere higher in Great Britain'.

The walk had taken about five hours, that was a decent average and I had a smoke to celebrate! The descent was tougher, particularly on the knees. Rocks had to be negotiated sideways, the terrain was slippery due to moss and the general climate, great care was needed. About half-way down, I took a breather and noticed a lady struggling with her right boot, blisters had paid her a visit. I stepped into the breach and carried her equipment down to the bottom, always keen to help! Once back on ground level, I gulped tea from my flask and bought ice cream from the van, they did a roaring trade from hill walkers. Sitting, having a good rest, I began to take in what I had achieved.

On returning to my hotel, I rang my parents to let them know I was safe, they were pleased and proud in equal measure.

That evening I bumped into Wayne, the chief instructor, and was enthusing about my day. Although very tired, the adrenaline was still pumping, and I said, 'Thank you so much, what a great event in aid of charity, it was mind-blowing'. He replied, 'Well done mate, you are very welcome, we aim to please.'

Following some nourishment, we were presented with a certificate each to mark our efforts.

Then crashed out for much-needed sleep, it had been both exhilarating and exhausting.

The next day I admired Ben Nevis as the coach departed from Fort William, promising myself a return visit one day.

The journey was tedious, I slept through much of it. Finally, we arrived at Brent Cross in London and I took the Tube back to Morden.

During the coming weeks the sponsor money was collected and sent to the charity, they acknowledged the donation with a letter of thanks which was appreciated.

Time passed by, and the following summer I went back for another crack at that beautiful mountain, the zest for it was addictive. A friend of mine from the club, James 'Taff' Davies, joined me for the adventure. He had served in the Royal Marines for the Redcap regiment, earning his nickname there having Welsh heritage in his bloodline.

Sadly, a medical discharge curtailed his Army career; witness to six of his division being murdered by the Taliban put paid to that.

Taff, as he preferred to be called, loved cider and could drink anyone under the table. I swear he had hollow legs! We sunk a few the night before our trek, missed the alarm call and had to bolt down breakfast.

Once on the trail, Taff had the solution; we would *yomp* up Ben Nevis, *yomping* being the Army term for a quick walk. He said, 'Come on J.C., best foot forward, let's march!' I laughed and replied, 'Yes Sir!'

It had been a while since I'd been addressed by my nickname, and as we set off, I remembered dear Miss Field from my primary school, wondering what she would have made of all this.

With great pride, I'm sure.

We soon caught up with our group and waved as we sailed by, hangovers never stopped us! No photos this time, the weather was poor, but a good time was had by all.

In 1996 I made it three in a row, Sarah was with me. I recalled with some mirth her comments about 'just striding up that hill', she barely broke sweat. It was great spending time with her again, we had a bond that would never be broken.

After arriving home, some very sad news was imparted to me. During my absence, my dear friend Roy had passed away following a sudden heart attack. He and Reg had been enjoying a beer whilst on a short break in Devon, there had been no warning signs as Roy appeared to be in fine fettle.

His funeral took place at North-East Surrey Crematorium in Garth Road, Lower Morden, Surrey. Many of his Fleet Street work colleagues attended, together with his friends from the club where the wake was held.

We all raised a glass to Roy. Rest in peace, my great mate.

Reality soon kicked in, back to the daily grind. I sought solace at the club, my place of refuge in good times and bad. It was a poignant moment as I looked at the empty seat next to me; I really missed my dear friend Roy, we shared many beers and laughs together, and went to Wembley to see our team cover themselves in glory. He gave me sound advice and was an all-round good bloke.

I had to re-set my mind, there was some serious thinking to be done. Life had become too predictable, the escapism of my recent trip being the exception. While waiting at the bar, I found myself engaged in conversation with a chap called Les Hill, a local painter and decorator, who was seeking an assistant to join him. Seizing the moment, I stated that I was available.

'Have you any experience in the trade?' Les enquired. Quick as a flash, I replied, 'No, but I'm very eager to learn.' He agreed to start me on a trial basis, that was good enough for me so I quit my job the following day. Goodbye to betting shops and good riddance.

To begin with, I dumped rubbish in skips and learnt how to prime wood, worked out which grade of sandpaper to use. As Dad always said, if you fail to prepare then prepare to fail. How true to life, not just decorating!

Over the course of time Les taught me well, we had many comedy moments along the way, cracking jokes and crying with laughter. I actually looked forward to work each day. Seeing the end product from a room in disrepair exuded much satisfaction.

We established a fruitful working relationship, and in August 2000 I gained a City and Guilds decorating certificate. It didn't come easy. I attended evening classes at Richmond College, based in Twickenham, every Thursday for three months, that after a long working day. You reap what you sow, as the saying goes.

Les and I continued in the same vein, the word had spread and good publicity was like finding gold dust. I also undertook some private work and built up a decent client base, felt like my niche in life had been found. It reached the point that I could almost paint in my sleep, the quality was that good.

Despite all that success, I had started to become anxious and could sense a disturbance in the ether around me. This was unsettling, given the lack of clarity as to what that was regarding.

Suddenly I felt vulnerable, and needed help to deal with these feelings. A very useful tool to assist me in this quest was shortly going to present itself, and transform my way of coping with adversity.

CHAPTER 8
Personal Development

Membership of the self-preservation society had made me acutely aware of threats out there; people with caveman mentality, and no thoughts about the consequences of their actions, just flailing fists and grunting noises. The incident at Cinatra's nightclub several years previously was a classic example of that, intimidation was their greatest weapon. I had put that episode to the back of my mind, however, it was now haunting me in the guise of flashbacks which I found unnerving. This was interrupting my train of thought both at work and socially, becoming an embarrassment that apologies were needed for.

One Sunday lunchtime in March 2003, I was sat in my usual seat near the bar. The match was a boring affair, nothing much happening, akin to a kickabout in the park. Then Taff strolled in (Remember Ben Nevis?) and ordered his 'pint of hairy spider', which in Cockney rhyming slang translated to pint of cider! He was a 3rd Dan black belt in Choi Kwang Do, a martial art of Korean origin, and Grandmaster Kwang Jo Choi developed this between 1978 and 1987. Proven to be the most effective in the world, this martial art involved the training of body and mind under the banners of mental discipline. The motto is 'Pil Sung', which means certain victory. Not in an aggressive manner, more of the mind, never give up or allow the spirit to be broken.

Taff regularly tried to encourage me to learn this self-defence art but to no avail, drinking booze was more my thing; negativity was in my head, too scared to try.

Eventually, the realisation that life could not be viewed through the bottom of a beer glass spurred me into action, and I attended a class one Tuesday evening. These were held at David Lloyd health and fitness club, Raynes Park. I had often been past there, never dreaming I would do anything like this; it just goes to show that you never know what is round the corner.

Walking in, I was greeted by Vince Cassar, who ran the academy. He explained the standards expected from every student. After being measured for my training uniform, I observed from the side, awestruck by the techniques on display. Taff was delighted I had taken the plunge into the unknown, he was aware of my issues and we had the obligatory drink afterwards.

Later that week I visited my parents for a few days, and on revealing my new venture they were pleased with my eagerness to try a different activity. Both appeared to be in good health, albeit ageing somewhat. I also made time to see my mate Tracy, who lived in Southfields, a district of inner London located near Wimbledon Common. We had become good friends and she was an important part of my support network.

At my first proper session, I was given a beginner's white belt and taught a basic pattern, this being to stand in right hand stance and execute an outwards block with my arm. The rule of thumb was to look forward and not at the floor, thus always keeping eyes on the threat and taking away the advantage from the opponent. This was repeated in left hand stance, then four-directional to cover all angles of attack. The advice was to defend myself as if I was in a phone box, in other words, a limited space on the street at close quarters.

There were thirty students in my class and I soon got to know them well, the etiquette being to bow and say, 'Pil Sung Sir', or Ma'am.

This signaled respect to each other, something lacking in the wider world, a sad indictment of modern society.

Training continued, my first grading was upon me, Vince was seated at a table to adjudicate. The Choi Kwang Do banner displayed prominently behind him. I duplicated what was taught to me, and then bowed. He said, 'Well done Mr. Carter, you performed very well.' I replied, 'Thank you Sir.' That was a good result, my willing attitude was shining through, though I had to keep pushing myself to make further headway, as my anxiety manifested itself randomly. Mastering moves such as claw strike, spinning side kick and rear elbow strike were all part of the curriculum, and after about a year I was helping new students just starting off.

Within the complex there was a massage studio, I reckoned I deserved to be pampered, so one day enquiries were made. A striking blonde German lady named Ingrid was in charge, she offered full body treatment with oils, scented candles and soft music. My slot was booked for the following evening, and to say this was a wonderful experience didn't do it justice. I was laid down, draped in a towel, totally relaxed as Ingrid went to work on my groins. It was impossible not to be aroused, and she knew that, it was plainly obvious due to my towel not laying flat anymore. At the conclusion, she said, 'I'm pleased you enjoyed our session Jon, would you like any extras?'

'Does a bear shit in the woods?' I smiled, and replied, 'It would be rude not to.' She then produced a condom and straddled me, we both made it to the line. What an unexpected bonus that was! I kept that part to myself but recommended the service to all and sundry, Ingrid always gave me the thumbs up as I left training.

Fitness drills were a major factor in my ascent up the martial arts ladder; we paired up using a large padded bag like in a boxing gym. One used hand and foot technique, then swapped over. Protection equipment was worn, safety in class was the watchword.

While practising this routine, I suffered an anxiety attack and had to stop abruptly. Shaking with fear, I headed for the changing rooms and cried my eyes out. Taff was first on the scene and gave me some water, he removed my protection gear and sat next to me.

'What's the problem, J.C.?' he asked. I couldn't speak, my throat had closed up. When the class finished, he dropped me home, we all looked out for each other. Regrettably, this episode was repeated from time to time, I was unable to predict or control it.

My gradings still went well though, as time went by I was going in the right direction, and finally after three years of hard graft I was seeing the fruit of my labours. Brown belt status had been achieved, and at this point I trained at the rear of the class for a month, rehearsing everything I had been taught.

There was a change of venue for my big day, March 19th, 2006. Vince had to lease new premises, as room at the health club was no longer available. He lived in Monkleigh Road, Morden, his house backed onto Hillcross school where I had begun my education. Incredibly, my black belt grading took place in the very hall where I sat on the floor for assembly as a five-year-old child. That filled me with emotion. I could almost see Miss Field standing there willing me on. This was completely surreal. Lined up with five fellow students, we in turn strutted our stuff, all that practice had paid off and finally it was done.

Outside, I smoked a much needed fag, not exactly a great advert for fitness but I didn't care. The award of my belt took place the following Thursday, unbeknown to me the other students had collected theirs two days previously. I needed a rest so hadn't been that evening.

The class lined up as usual, myself in the back row. Vince stepped forward, and said, 'Before we begin tonight, we have one more belt to give out, namely to Mr. Carter. Sir, you have been on some journey to reach this point, it's not been smooth at times.' I smiled and replied, 'Thank you Sir, and everyone, for your support. I got there in the end.'

The belt was fastened around my waist, to rapturous applause. This was such a proud moment for me. I had persevered showing the indomitable spirit instilled in me, principally by my parents. They were my guiding light in everything I did and this was no different.

During the intervening years, I continued my training indoors once or twice a week, just to keep in the swim of it. Wearing the belt was an honour, however, my depression problem was still niggling away like a boil on the arse of humanity. My doctor suggested medication but I declined, instead relying on my own resources.

That said, a portent of unrest seemed to be hovering above, and I was about to face the most difficult period of my life so far.

CHAPTER 9

Tragedy

During the Spring of 2012 anticipation was growing for the forthcoming Olympic Games in London, inflation sat at around 2.8% and David Cameron was Prime Minister, leading a coalition with the Liberal Democrats. The usual political merry-go-round of rumours and denials were prevalent, keeping newspaper editors busy.

My work was going well, Les and I refurbished a large house, he loved wallpapering and was an expert in that field. I noticed a weight loss in him, nevertheless, he just ploughed on, never one to bother a doctor. He was bingo caller at the club every Friday night, followed by a huge fish and chip supper, and I used to stand at the bar mimicking him, two little ducks, twenty-two and so on. There was a vague semblance of normality in general, but this was about to change dramatically.

My Mother phoned me, the tone of her voice was different and quieter. She expressed concern about Dad, he had stumbled over in the hallway, thankfully sustaining no injuries. This was worrying, given that he was eighty-five with no previous balance issues. I reassured Mum that I would ring the next day to check on the situation, and advised her to call the emergency services if it happened again. This gave me food for thought. My parents were getting older and more vulnerable to accidents, so I notified their doctor who recorded the incident.

A few days later came another call. Mum was tense and upset as Dad had fallen over in the garden. She had wisely acted promptly, and paramedics were there in no time to take care of Dad and transport him to St. Richard's Hospital, which was thankfully nearby. Filled with frustration and concern, it dawned on me that I couldn't do much to help on the end of a phone, so I made a snap decision to relocate and live near my parents.

Instinct told me that something bad was brewing, so I put my property on the market and made preparations. Les agreed that family was priority, he would have done the same, so on April 2nd, 2012 I arrived in Chichester, renting a flat about five minutes walk from my parents' house. My relief was tangible, at least I was nearby to assist when needed, and as time went on this turned out to be the best move I ever made.

By this juncture, my Father was using a walking stick and we took short walks in the back garden, just to keep him active. He held my arm for support and was pleased I was now living in the area. This took the weight off Mum's shoulders. There was a hospital appointment to attend, I accompanied Dad by taxi. This was physiotherapy on his legs and lower back. He found this hard going, I could see it in his eyes, but persevered anyway and never complained. The stick was replaced with a walking frame, slow progress became a shuffle.

This proud upstanding man, six feet tall, the abiding image of my Father with his pomp, smiling when conducting the choir; now he was sadly a shadow of his former self. My poor Mother was bemused, not understanding why her husband of sixty-three years was becoming so ill. She was not able to process any of it. I supported her in every way possible, but in my mind was the realisation that this was only going to get worse.

'Careline' was installed, and Dad wore a pendant to press if he got into difficulties; mentally he was sharp as a tack so knew how to raise the alarm. I was the point of contact, and within a few days they had rung me at two o'clock in the morning. I quickly dressed and ran to the house, my heart was pounding.

After letting myself in with a spare key, I was confronted by a horrific scene; my Father was on the floor, helpless and struggling, laying in his own excrement. Realising he was choking, I cradled his head and cleared the airway. Dad's tongue was lodged in his throat. Having had no medical training, instinct kicked in and I managed to save his life. This had been truly awful for him. And traumatising for me.

After washing Dad and dressing him in clean pyjamas, I got him comfortable in his armchair and stayed by his side until morning broke. Mum came downstairs. She had been oblivious to all of this. The doctor paid a visit, and told me that without my intervention it could have been fatal.

Shortly afterwards, Dad showed me a letter from his Consultant. It made for grim reading. Suffice to say, he was suffering from a condition known as *Apraxia*, a neurological disorder that makes it difficult or impossible to perform learned movement, even when the person wants to do it.

In layman's terms, the brain sends a signal but it stops short of the limbs, thus causing falls. The final line of the letter stated there was nothing more they could do, which was devastating for my Father.

We had a hug, and Dad said, 'Jon, I know my time is short, please make sure that Mum is kept safe and looked after.' I looked into his eyes that were moistening, and replied, 'Dad, I promise you faithfully that Mum will never come to any harm, and I will guard her with my life.' This was an emotional moment for us both.

I felt so desperately upset that this fine, selfless man, the glue that held our family together, was now fading fast. Soon, he was back in hospital, sadly deteriorating. Mum and I were there at his bedside, my poor Father was crying and saying how much he loved us both. I bent down to kiss him and my tears were falling onto his face, he was thrashing about on his bed, shouting *'No more, no more.'* This was terminal agitation. I could not bear to see this so I ordered the nurse to prepare morphine, which was administered without delay.

The hospital staff provided an inflatable bed, I was not going anywhere and stayed with Dad that night and all the following day. Sleep was not happening, and numerous excursions for fags were required to keep me going. Each time I returned, my Dad's breathing was more shallow. Sitting by the bed, holding his hand, I heard his heart stop, and then restart. Then his heart stopped. On the evening of Friday 29th November 2013 my beloved Father passed away peacefully.

The nurses were enormously supportive and helpful, doing what they were trained for. I returned and broke the news to Mum. Although the outcome was inevitable that did not lessen the blow. I embraced her, and we cried together.

My Mother could not bring herself to see her husband at the Chapel of Rest, so I went alone. There was Dad laying there, his spirit departed, looking peaceful and calm. No more agitation and stress. I took some comfort from that.

Following instructions in his Will, Dad was cremated at Chichester Crematorium. Of his friends who were still alive, some did attend. I read out a speech highlighting his devotion to Mum, commitment to family values, and his love of church music. I stood proudly as the service concluded with *'Zadok the Priest'*, a musical arrangement he once played on the organ. Goodbye, dear Father, my Hero.

The ensuing days and weeks were fraught with emotion. Christmas was cancelled, no cards were sent, we received condolence messages and just took things one day at a time. Mum's eyes were red raw, she dealt with the loss in her own way, preferring to grieve privately.

Then one morning, I made my Mother a coffee and we sat chatting about Dad. Suddenly, she lurched forwards clutching her stomach, screaming in pain, and her chair tilted backwards towards the glass cabinet that housed the fine crockery. I got there just in time, preventing her head from smashing into the glass frontage.

Mum was white as a sheet and her eyes were rolling. The thought raced through my mind that I was going to lose both parents in a short space of time. I dialled for an ambulance and it arrived, light flashing. They took Mum in and it was diagnosed that she had a dormant tumour in her bowel, the shock of losing Dad had triggered it. And even worse, it was cancerous. I started to think there was a curse on us. Kicking when we were at our lowest ebb.

An operation was carried out, Mum displaying her dominant stoic nature. She sailed through it, wondering what all the fuss was about!

Once back home, plenty of bed rest was the order of the day, and gradually my Mother recovered. I was praying that the cancer would not spread and one day the surgeon confirmed there was no indication of that at the present time. I stayed at Mum's side at all times. I was her son and carer, honoured to be so.

One day, Mum said, 'Thank you for everything you are doing for me Jon. I wouldn't be here if it wasn't for you.' I put my arm around her shoulder, and replied, 'It's a pleasure Mum, I will always look after you.' That conversation was worth its weight in gold.

In July 2014 we got a dog from the Dogs Trust, who were based in Shoreham, West Sussex. I thought this was a good idea, hoping a pet would bring some stability, and company for both of us. The animal in question was a black and white Jack Russell Terrier, and we named him Jack. He was ten years old, and had lived a somewhat chequered life thus far, re-homing had been an issue due to his boisterous nature. However, once he had settled in, there was a transformation. No outside walks as Jack had some issues with other dogs; instead, our large back garden was his kingdom, and he loved it.

I used to observe as Mum pottered about, Jack right by her side keeping an eye on proceedings. He felt loved, and that was reciprocated. Hiding his Dentine sticks under cushions in the lounge was a favourite game to play, then barking, daring us to try and find them! I often peered round the doorway to see Jack asleep on Mum's lap, what a lovely sight.

It was very heartwarming to see Mum smile again, after all that pain. Maybe now there was a chink of light?

Our beautiful dog had Dad's brown eyes, and I know my Father was looking down on his darling wife with approval.

Sometimes, it was nigh on impossible to move forward after such a huge loss. There were some days when I felt like I was walking through treacle, and it was the same for Mum. My anxiety levels were rising, and I was experiencing flashbacks about the distressing scenes I had witnessed.

Looking at my Father's empty armchair really hit it home, to the extent that I hardly ever left the house, save for buying shopping. I could feel his presence, like he was guiding me through this tumultuous time; without any doubt, Dad was carrying me on his shoulders. We carried on as best we could, given the circumstances.

Mum's sister Doris came down for a few days, it was good to see them together, swapping memories over cups of tea. In time, I even managed to take on the task of decorating at our local church, *St. Wilfrid's* in Sherbourne Road, where my parents attended when they moved to the area. It was pleasing to do some work, despite feeling under par.

I took Mum into town for a cream tea, and afterwards we sat by the Cathedral, reflecting on life in general. All felt reasonably calm, however, I was about to face some huge challenges in the near future.

Dark clouds were gathering, once again, to test my mettle. This was relentless, and it was starting to feel like I had done something wrong in a previous life, and was being punished. I was going to have to stand stronger than ever, and keep my Mother safe.

CHAPTER 10
Protecting Mum

Drawing on my mental resources was essential to provide a stable environment and care for my Mother. I had been traumatised when I found Dad on the floor, and was determined that history would not repeat itself. Despite having no formal training as a carer, I was thankfully blessed with common sense; with that in mind, the correct procedure was to walk behind Mum as she walked upstairs, and step backwards in front of her on the descent. There were handrails on both sides to assist in this. I had helped Dad install them.

My Mother was just about still able to slowly bend and pick up weeds. She took great pride in the garden and the great array of flowers on show, with pots standing to attention in neat rows. We often sat out on the garden bench, Jack in between us, his favourite pastime was to nibble on the fruitcake we enjoyed with our tea! Mum often spotted butterflies hovering near plants and bushes, they seemed to bring an air of tranquility and innocence from another world. I helped with Doctor and hospital appointments, it was noticeable that age was creeping up on her, like it does for us all.

As Mum was an asthma sufferer, I made sure the pumps were used every day. Sitting opposite until satisfied. Some ingenious tricks were to conceal pills down the back of cushions, and pour energy drinks into flowerpots. Staying vigilant was key! Furniture walking was starting to feature, the term used when holding onto a chair or doorframe. This caused me concern, I made sure she rested and took it easy.

One day, Mum instigated a conversation about the house, stating that it would be a good idea to register ownership in both our names.

She said, 'I think that is sensible in case anything happens to me, you are an outstanding son and I know Dad would agree.' We duly arranged to see our solicitors, and the transfer was ratified. Additionally, I was appointed as Lasting Power of Attorney to oversee affairs relating to Property and Finance, together with Health and Welfare.

This was a huge undertaking. I was the last line of defence and would literally do anything to protect her.

During the early months of 2017, I looked at the situation and moved in permanently. Being there all the time anyway, this made logical sense. Breaking the rental agreement on my flat didn't go down too well, but so what. Mum was now using a walking frame so I needed to be with her, simple as that.

One afternoon the dog groomer arrived to give Jack a makeover, clip his nails and so forth. Our pet wasn't keen and took much persuasion to emerge from behind the sofa. Food did the trick as usual. When the treatment had finished, the groomer commented on the fact that Jack was looking a bit grey around the gills, and there was a thicker waistline on show. Unsurprising really, given that he was now thirteen.

Tracy from Southfields got in touch, we had not spoken for a while and had a good catch-up. There was a new man in her life who treated her with respect, unlike a previous partner who was a narcissist bully and used to beat her. The domestic violence was a cowardly form of control, the individual concerned now had a permanent limp, nobody did that to my friend!

Jack always slept upstairs with Mum. I had swapped the double mattress for a single, thus making it easier for him to get on the bed. He snuggled up next to Mum, even had his own pillow.

On the 18th May, the day before my birthday, I popped him into the garden as usual while I made his breakfast, and a cup of tea for Mum. The kettle had not even boiled when I heard a loud shriek — Jack was slowly making his way back towards me, his left rear leg just hanging.

Initially, I thought there was an issue with the pads on his feet, he was forever licking them. On closer inspection the reality hit me: he was lame and could not walk. I cried the first of a million tears for him. After settling him in the lounge on a blanket, I got Mum downstairs safely and we sat with Jack.

It was Saturday, but I managed to contact an emergency vet who dispensed painkillers. It was tricky administering them, but eventually Jack accepted scrambled eggs with a crushed tablet. I blocked the stairs and turned the chairs around to try and discourage him from trying to jump up. His favourite place was Mum's lap, and he could not understand why he had to stay on the floor. The poor soul thought he had misbehaved. It was so sad. Jack was so unhappy, I could see it in his brown eyes, like Dad looking back at me.

An operation was suggested by the veterinary surgeon. Mum and I discussed it and decided the risk was too great, given his age. For sixteen days and nights I stayed with Jack on the floor, guarding him against further damage to his leg. It nearly killed me, hardly sleeping a wink — just holding him close to me, hearing his sighs at regular intervals.

Finally, we took the option of euthanasia. Watching him suffer was unbearable. On Monday 5th June, two vets came to the house, it was a quick and painless procedure, the right course of action for him.

My Mother wept uncontrollably, this was too much for her. It all felt so unfair, we never seemed to get the rub of the green with anything. Later that day I said to Mum that part of me went with him. That was borne out, as I never recovered from the trauma.

That evening, the sky turned dark at about six o'clock and I heard a bark outside the front door. As we all know our own pets' noises, I was convinced it was Jack. I went outside but he wasn't there. As a strong believer in the spirit world, I knew he was saying goodbye at that moment.

This tragic event left a terrible sense of loss; I did my best for Mum but we just sat there in silence for days on end, staring into space. For a long time I was weeping down my phone to the Dogs Trust bereavement counsellor, the feeling of guilt tearing me apart. Of course, I had done nothing wrong, and they explained to me that this was a common emotion within the grieving process that faced pet owners.

Then one day, I was sitting alone in the garden when I saw Jack in my mind's eye, there he was, jumping about in a field with four good legs. That was his message to me that all was good and he was safe at Rainbow Bridge, which to the initiated is 'Doggy Heaven'. I saw him many times after that, such as a shape moving in the corner of a room. His collar and lead are with me to this day, together with his water bowl. I retained a lovely photo of Jack on Mum's lap, taken when we first acquired him as our pet. I always admire that picture, and say to him: *'Good boy, look after your Mummy.'*

He certainly did that, and still does from above.

God bless you Jack, we will love you forever.

So there we were, with no dog. Poor Mum had the same look in her eyes when Dad passed away. It was raw, and hurt like hell. Jack had a great three years with us, but now there was a massive void. The garden felt empty, we sat there hoping he would appear from behind a bush, wagging his tail, but of course that was wishful thinking.

Then one morning, Mum and I were seated at the dining table, sipping coffee amid stoney silence. I made a comment about the weather, Mum just stared at me and her face had dropped to one side. Having watched medical programmes on television, I knew immediately that this was the sign of a possible stroke. I dialled for help, holding her tight at the same time. Mum was ashen-faced and attempting to speak but no words were forthcoming.

She was taken to hospital and placed in intensive care. Thank goodness I had moved from London to be near my parents, or she might have died that day.

By the summer of 2018 my Mother was becoming more frail. She had withstood all those dreadful ordeals, and shown great stoicism which typified her generation. They went through a World War and extreme hardship, unlike the present day when people complained about the rain and compared that to a nightmare. I beg to differ, a nightmare was where bombs were falling and there was no food to eat.

Events came to a head when I popped out for a newspaper and returned to find Mum on the floor. Although thankfully never badly injured, she was now struggling to keep her balance. By this time, my own health had been impacted; the physical and mental stress was taking its toll. This was not because of Mum, she was good as gold, never asking for anything or complaining; it was the culmination of me dealing with such traumatic situations that led me to take her to our doctor. I pointed out that if I went under, then Mum would need to be looked after. He spoke to my Mother, with me present, and it was agreed that in the interests of her welfare she would be safer in a Care Home. I had done my absolute best, this was the sensible option. The doctor was very helpful — furnishing me with details of local care facilities, useful as I didn't know where to start. I rang Marriot Lodge, a residential home in Tolhouse Lane, Chichester, which unbeknown to me was a few minutes walk away, tucked away from the main road near the college. An appointment was made to meet the Manager on the following day. After being shown around the site, the costs of care were explained to me and Mum was given a month of respite care, beginning straight away. It was difficult explaining to her that she would not be living in her own house during that trial period. After all those years living there with Dad, sadly that was now history.

On my first visit Mum was sitting on the bed in her room, bags packed, asking when she could come home. She said, 'I don't like it here Jon, I want to be in my own house and sit in my garden.' That was an awkward moment, and I replied, 'It will be alright Mum, I appreciate that this is all new to you, but rest assured I am only round the corner and will visit regularly.' She smiled, patting my hand, and we spent some time looking at old photographs I had brought in. We sat on a bench outside and admired the neat row of manicured conifer bushes, together with colourful hanging baskets of flowers. Carers were buzzing to and fro, going about their daily routine.

During that respite month, Social Services from West Sussex County Council carried out a Deprivation of Liberty assessment on my Mother; this was standard procedure for all new residents, to ascertain whether they were there of their own free will. On being satisfied with Mum, she was then given a permanent placement, much to my relief. As joint owner of our house I continued to live there, keeping the place shipshape and carrying out maintenance where needed. Our home felt really empty, and I often reflected on all that had gone before. Over the course of time Mum settled down well, the Home was a safe environment and she received twenty-four hour care. Friendships were forged, activities to join in if she wanted to. Scrabble was a favourite pastime, and it helped keep her brain active, she and Dad used to play every Monday evening and tot up the scores. Dad was very adept at finding triple letters, this really frustrated Mum! All seemed well, she looked happier and it warmed my heart to see this. Now and again I stayed for lunch, the food was good and wine was on the menu to wet the palate. One female carer caught my attention, old habits die hard. I was only human. Off limits though, they were not allowed to fraternise with relatives of residents. Never mind. Can't win them all! On the occasions Mum had been in hospital, in particular when she suffered a stroke, tests on her brain had been carried out to ascertain whether any lasting damage had been done. Her memory was starting to fade, repetition becoming an everyday occurrence. The hospital rang to inform me that a medical consultant wanted to see Mum and I at the home, this was scheduled for January 14th 2019. The poignancy was not lost on me, that date was my Father's birthday. The meeting began and I listened intently as their findings were read out to me. The diagnosis was the onset of Alzheimers and Dementia, together with cognitive impairment due to the stroke. Alzheimers disease is a progressive brain disorder that slowly destroys the memory and impacts the ability to carry out simple tasks. Although I had suspected this outcome for some time, it was very hard to process, and Mum did not really understand what was being said. My mind floated back to when Dad told me about his apraxia condition, and when the meeting concluded I went home to contemplate the days events.

Armed with this information, some hard thinking was needed. Unfortunately, it was plain to see that this situation was only going to worsen, and my Mother might well require some specialist nursing in the future. This was going to incur huge costs. Currently the fees were five thousand a month anyway, which Mum was paying from her savings and pension.

There was no bottomless pit of money, so only one option was available to me. I needed to protect Mum at all costs, as I promised my Father. When I next went to see her, we sat in her room and I discussed my thinking, this being that the house had to be sold to raise funds for care fees. My Mother said, 'I can't see that being a problem Jon, do what you need to do.' As Lasting Power of Attorney, I was legally required to act in the interests of the Donor, this being Mum, which is what I did forthwith. This was never about me owning a nice house one day, in the cold light of day that was just bricks and mortar. My Mother's welfare was paramount, so the property was sold and we shared the proceeds. I know, without doubt, that my dear Dad approved of my actions. A great burden lifted off my shoulders, and I rented a small flat close to the home; it was vital to remain nearby. Visits continued, then one day I noticed a change in Mum's appearance. There had been a tiny red spot on her left cheek many years earlier, at the time the Dermatologist specialist had stated there was nothing to cause concern. Now however, a lump was forming, to the extent that the care staff were alarmed about it. By now, Mum was in a wheelchair and too frail to travel, so the hospital Facial unit looked at images sent by our Doctor. These confirmed skin cancer, and an operation was hastily arranged. I had to make a monumental decision with the surgeon. As

Attorney, the paperwork had to be signed by me to proceed; my Mother was ninety-one and about to go under general anaesthetic. I prayed and took a leap of faith. In September 2019 the operation went ahead with my authority. I spent all day there, pacing up and down outside, a total nervous wreck. My trusty roll-ups featured heavily, whatever your views on smoking, they certainly helped me in times of stress. After what felt like an eternity, I was allowed into the recovery room, and there was my dear Mother sitting up and diving into tea and biscuits. She looked at me and said, 'Oh, hello Jon, how nice to see you, what are you doing here then?' A truly remarkable lady, nothing fazed her. I smiled and held her hand, saying, 'I love you Mum.' Following a delay with the transport, we finally arrived back at Marriot House at about ten in the evening. The night staff made Mum comfortable and I went home. She slowly made progress, and at Christmas we had lunch together, enjoying the entertainment by a singer. I felt Dad's presence as Mum clapped her hands to the music, it had been a joyous day.

A new decade beckoned. Britain left the European Union, a huge mistake in my opinion. There was tension between America and Iran, together with major bushfires in Australia which claimed many lives. A stabbing attack in Paris was another stark headline, any right-minded person never understood the motives behind such an atrocity. There were rumours of a virus affecting China, but nobody here took much notice, the mindset being that it was not in our backyard. Unbeknown to us all, however, a calamity of seismic proportions was about to engulf our planet, the likes of which had never been seen in modern times.

CHAPTER 11
Global Crisis

The advent of Spring was on the horizon, daffodils were adding colour after what had been a bleak winter, and the odour of freshly cut grass hung in the air. I did my weekly shopping and needed the Hubble Telescope to read the sell-by dates on products, why manufacturers printed them so small was beyond me! Visits to Mum continued, she was settled and content, albeit inside a dementia bubble. Folk were going about their daily business, oblivious to the drama that was about to unfold.

It was just a normal evening as I watched the usual boring television programmes, playing roulette with the remote control, and wondered if a rebate for the licence fee might be in the offing. Suddenly, the routine was interrupted by a news bulletin at about eight o'clock. Our Prime Minister Boris Johnson addressed the nation, giving us all one simple instruction; there was an outbreak of Covid-19, a dangerous respiratory virus that was claiming lives, and we had to stay at home. He further pointed out that our National Health Service was in danger of being overwhelmed and we should all stay vigilant. It was hard to process all this information. I just sat there stunned as I'm sure the whole country did. On 23rd March 2020 life as we knew it changed forever, we were in lockdown. The streets were deserted, like a scene from a science fiction movie, rolls of tumbleweed would not have looked out of place, it was totally bizarre. Ministers were reciting speeches and showing graphs indicating the rise in infection rates, shops were empty, save for food. Queue two metres apart and wear a face mask were the requirements we all had to adhere to. Visits to Care Homes were severely restricted, before each visit I did a test for the virus, considering that to be my moral responsibility. The Government displayed staggering incompetence by releasing hospital patients back to that environment before they had been tested, thus leading to hundreds of unnecessary deaths. My Mother tested positive, thankfully showing no symptoms; as she was asthmatic I feared the worst, but Mum flatly refused to be taken by any form of illness.

The first few weeks of lockdown were very strange, there was much speculation as to how long this might last, hoping it would just blow over. To alleviate the boredom I drew up a plan, this being to shed some weight and train for an hour or so on alternate days. I was very thankful that I knew a martial art, all that experience held me in good stead. Another way to pass the time was to do crosswords. This kept my brain active. All that said, my anxiety and depression was worsening, it was starting to feel like the walls were closing in. One day, out of nowhere, I picked up a writing pad and began documenting my life story. A few pages here and there then back in the drawer. That is when my idea of writing a book began. A year passed, and vaccines offered a way forward, but there was a general feeling of wariness and caution. I ceased going to the pub for fear of getting infected, my overwhelming priority was to protect my Mother so if that meant isolating myself then so be it. The downside to that, of course, was a gradual decline in my health, so I booked an appointment to see a doctor. Clarissa Young worked at Parklands Surgery, Chichester as a locum general practitioner, and she gave me forty minutes of her time as I unloaded my tales of distress. During our conversation, the writing I had begun got a mention. She looked pleased, and said, 'That is a very good tool to use in respect of your well-being, if you ever get published please send me a copy.' I smiled, replying, 'Well, you never know'. Anti-depressants were duly dispensed, not really my thing as I didn't use medication, but something had to be done so I relented. When turning on the radio, it was announced that the authorities were now testing elderly patients in hospital before sending them back to Care homes; a classic case of 'after the horse has bolted', so much so that the stable door was flapping in the wind.

Never on one occasion was it imparted to Mum that I had health issues, the worry would have been too much for her and I didn't want to disrupt the equilibrium that was in place. On every visit I smiled and carried on as normal, not revealing my inner turmoil that was eating away at me. Poor Mum seemed to age ten years over one weekend. I barely recognised her and that was extremely upsetting. However, the sternest challenge that I ever faced in my life was about to manifest itself and test my resolve to the absolute limit, threatening my very existence.

CHAPTER 12

On The Brink

As the world rolled into 2023, restrictions had eased somewhat, the general concensus being to try and get on with life, and not dwell on recent events; the pandemic had scythed through virtually every country claiming at least three million lives globally, nothing would ever be normal again. Economies were left reeling and torn to shreds, prices of goods were sky high. This created its own problems. My Mother was by now hardly eating her meals, she never had a big appetite, instead relying on fortified energy milk drinks. I came up with the idea of giving her chocolate buttons, which were small and melted in her mouth, at least this was some nourishment. Mum loved these and saw them as a treat, but sadly due to the destructive nature of Alzheimer's disease, she had the quirks of her childhood. One day, Mum said, 'I really like the sweets, may I have another one please?' Such a kind gentle lady, very often after a visit I was reduced to tears. Sarah came down to see me, it was wonderful to hug my soul mate again. She could sense that I was struggling to hold it all together, and gave me her full support as always. We went for a walk along Chichester canal towpath, chatting and reminiscing.

Life continued in the same vein until one morning in April, when I awoke to be confronted by a force of evil. The bedroom was spinning, perspiration drenching my body. In my mind's eye I was reliving terrible traumatic moments, like finding Dad on the floor and saying goodbye to Jack. An hour or so later I managed to get up, made a cup of tea and sat shaking with fear. To say I was confused did not even cut it, eventually phoning my surgery in a cry for help.

To be fair, they took me seriously and I was seen by a doctor that afternoon. Having previously highlighted my anxiety issues, I was referred to 'Talking Therapies' for an assessment. This service from the N.H.S dealt with mental health issues including trauma, but I was on a long waiting list, the sad reality being that many people suffered from this condition. Three months later I was given an appointment with a therapist who threw numerous questions at me. I relayed the disturbing images that were playing through my mind like a film, it was an upsetting experience sitting with a complete stranger and blurting it all out. Based on the information given, it was confirmed that I was showing classic symptoms of Post Traumatic Stress Disorder (PTSD), these findings were sent to my doctor and stronger medication for me was recommended. While walking home I felt a sense of relief that I had been listened to; it took immense courage to step forward, that was the hardest part overcome but there were many difficult hurdles in front of me.

On December 4th of that year I attended the first of many sessions with my allocated therapist, whose name was Eleanor. By this point I was so fragile and confused, not even recognising my image in the mirror. I recall saying to myself, 'Where is the person I used to be, the old me?' I felt so isolated, like I didn't belong to anything; just falling down a rabbit hole with no way out, sliding into the abyss, I was at my lowest point, even contemplating taking my own life. I just could not go through with it though. Mum was the one person who kept me going and we had been through so much, she would not have survived without me. Eleanor and I sat down, and she said, 'Hi Jon, I can see from your assessment that you need urgent help. The first phase of treatment will be Trauma-Focused Cognitive Behavioral Therapy. Please feel free to ask any questions, there is no rush, just take your time.' I just stared into space only managing a token 'Thank you.' The essence of this was to focus on a picture hanging on a wall, and just concentrate on that area. Closed eyes and deep breathing, then repeat. She then asked me to identify a safe place in my life, where I had been calm and peaceful. I chose the slopes of Ben Nevis as the image in my mind, recalling how free and relaxed I felt on those previous trips.

We discussed my adoption, and Eleanor pointed out that being given up at birth was a common cause of childhood trauma affecting development in many cases. The area of the human brain called the Hippocampus processed trauma, and high levels of stress caused impaired function. This made some people more prone to PTSD, memories became stored in the wrong place, rather like a library with books misfiled. The sessions continued, and I was learning more about my health condition and the reasons behind it. Standing alone against the forces of darkness was my toughest assignment, it was me against the world. While having a rare quiet moment, I remembered a poem entitled 'Footprints'. This featured a man trudging through the sand and only seeing one set of prints, he cried out to God, saying, 'Where are you when I need you the most?' God explained that he was with the man, carrying him through the challenging moments of his life. I made the analogy that the reason I had survived was down to the fact that my Father was bearing my burden from above, guiding me in the right direction. No doubt about that whatsoever.

Another useful tool I learned of was a book called 'Make Your Bed' written by Admiral William H. McRaven, a former U.S. Navy Seal. He documented his experiences, highlighting the fact that if life was a struggle, then making your bed was the first achievement of the day, bringing a sense of calm. It was more beneficial to face down obstacles, rather than avoid them; for example, 'Talking Therapies' were helping me to 'paddle the boat', so to speak. I wasn't doing that alone. It was crucial not to feel like the world was against me, and not live in fear of failure; to stand my ground even in the darkest moments, no matter how hard it got, and reach deep inside my soul to do my best. When Admiral McRaven was a recruit, there was a large bell hanging in the corner of the parade ground. Anyone who wanted to give up then had to ring the bell. The moral of this story being to always 'stand tall, rise above the pain' and never quit.

All of this really resonated with me. I was battling a tidal wave that was threatening to dismantle my mental health and destroy me. The loss of loved ones and our beloved pet Jack had taken so much out of me, I felt like the tank was empty. Then I remembered the courage and determination my dear Father had shown, not only during his lifetime but at the end as well. He had been my strength to fight against the odds and never ring that bell, the life lessons that he taught me were invaluable. I had continuously put my head above the parapet and taken all that was thrown at me, however, I was going to have to dig deep once more to absorb the calamity that was soon to unfold, and be too much to bear.

CHAPTER 13

End of an Era

At a certain point in all our lives came a time when changes occurred that we could not control, that was just the way events unfolded, all mapped out in advance. We went about our daily trudgery, blissfully unaware of what lay ahead, this gave some variety to existing. Imagine knowing what was going to happen beforehand, that would have been somewhat robotic in nature.

In February 2024, news reached me from London that my Mother's sister Doris had passed away following a stay in hospital. Although my Auntie was not a blood relative of mine there was still a sense of loss, and I now had to tell Mum, breaking it to her gently. She looked a bit shocked but I could tell that the ravages of Dementia indicated to me that the information was not registering. Mum said, 'That's a shame, I will say a prayer for her,' and then proceeded to chat about the weather. This appeared to be a defence mechanism. I recalled similar mannerisms when her dear husband Dennis died. As Lasting Power of Attorney for the Health and Welfare of my Mother, I sensibly deemed that she was far too frail and unwell to travel all that way for the service, instead I arranged for the committal to be streamed live to the Care Home. We sat together in front of a screen, my dear Mum oblivious to the proceedings, at least I had tried my best in honour of her sister.

As the year wore on my time spent at Marriot Lodge increased dramatically. I had put in place that there were to be no hospital trips whatsoever, and Mum was to be given palliative care at the Home when that time arrived.

This felt like a juggling act as I was trying to manage my own health at the same time. No matter how rough I felt, being with my Mother was priority, pushing my own issues into the background. I rang my friend Steve who joined me for a visit, he had met Mum many years earlier when undertaking building repairs at the house. Unfortunately she did not recognise him, but it was good to have some moral support. By this stage Mum was too weak to be moved from her bed to a wheelchair, and on voicing my concerns to the head carer Christina, she said, 'We all love Joyce, sadly this is the circle of life with old age, she is comfortable in her room and will be checked on at regular intervals.' I went outside to the bench where Mum and I had sat so many times drinking tea and just being together. Sitting head in hands, I drew heavily on a cigarette, my eyes moistening. The following day I rang to check on her and she said, 'I'm alright Jon, I've just been talking to Doris.' This was the tipping point when I realised the end was on the horizon. A visitation from her sister was a message, like a calling to the other side. My Mother's condition deteriorated to the point where she was asleep all the time and not taking nourishment, it was looking bleak. The local vicar was summoned and he administered the last rites at her bedside, tears were streaming down my face as I held Mum's hand for the final time. That evening I went home and prepared myself for the worst. Sleep was impossible, cups of tea were consumed, many cigarettes smoked, I sat and admired the black and white photograph hanging on my wall, which depicted my parents wedding day back in 1950; such a wonderful picture of two people setting off on the path of married life together.

What happened next absolutely stunned me. There was my Mother, standing and smiling at me. As a staunch believer in the spiritual world I knew this was the moment when she came to say goodbye.

For half an hour or so, I walked up and down the room feeling joyous and exhilarated.

At two o'clock the following morning, on Monday 25th November 2024, I received a phone call from the night staff at the Care Home, my dear Mother had slipped away peacefully in her sleep. I just sat on my bed, numb with grief. Although this news was inevitable at some stage, it was like a hammer blow like no other. I took some solace from the fact that Mum was now free and reunited with my Dad. Walking to the Care Home was slow and arduous; my legs felt like lead weights and I was in a bubble of emotion, no outside noise was audible. When I arrived, Christina hugged me and some carers were crying, they were all a family and felt the loss when losing a resident. On entering Mum's room there was just an empty bed, it did not seem real. I stood there and said a prayer for her. The next port of call was Oakland's Funeral Services, a short walk from the Home. They expressed their condolences and we discussed the options available, I had done the same for Dad back in 2013 so I knew the ropes so to speak, but that didn't make the task any less painful. In her Will, my Mother stated the wish to be cremated so the Crematorium was the chosen venue. I selected black Friesian horses to draw a white carriage, together with a beautiful white coffin for Mum. When I recall the very moving moments as our late Queen was taken to Westminster Abbey, the procession music was to be the same, this being The Mist Covered Mountains of Home. Only the best for My Mother, as she was my Queen. A bagpiper was also selected to accompany the cortège. My mate Steve attended to support me, I felt alone and helpless. We were both dressed to the nines, complete with Peaky Blinders caps, and I wore one of Dad's ties so it felt like he was with me.

The proudest and saddest day of my life was on 16th December 2024 when I led my dear Mother up Sherborne Road, Chichester towards the Crematorium. Louise the undertaker walked alongside me, with John the piper leading, playing that wonderful music. Total respect was shown, cars stopped at the roadside, people took photographs. My mouth was dry with nerves but I stood tall to honour my Mum, and felt Dad was nearby. Music I chose for the service included 'It Must be Love', sung by Labi Siffre, for a visual life tribute showing pictures of Mum and her sister along with images of my parents together. The final hymn was 'All Things Bright and Beautiful', selected by my Father. He had written his wishes on paperwork I had discovered and kept. There were also Bible readings that he chose. It was amazing that he was part of the service from up above. That filled me with immense pride. I made a speech, highlighting my Mother's dedication to family values, her love of gardening and cooking, and the stoic nature she showed at all times. Special thanks were given to the Care Home staff for keeping Mum safe and happy during the six years and four months she stayed there. Back in 1999 I wrote some poetry that was published, one of these being titled 'Mother', which I read out at the service. I felt this was a fitting tribute to my heroine, who gave everything to love and support me through good times and bad, selfless in all she did. The poem reads as follows:

She raised me and clothed me

Never once complaining,

Walked me to school every day

Even when it was raining,

Holidays to the seaside

And trips to the park,

Always having fun

And enjoying a lark.

As I grew up

Through my school years,

Mother was always there

With hopes and fears.

Starting work and meeting girls

Poor Mother's head really

Was in a whirl!

Leaving home and

Buying my own place,

I figured my Mother

Must need some space.

I know in my heart

There will never be another,

Because it is a fact

That I love my dear Mother.

For the Commendation and Farewell music, 'Songbird' by Christine McVie rang out as the curtains closed. This was a fitting send-off for my dear Mum, one she richly deserved after such a great life, reaching the age of ninety-six.

When I moved down to Chichester in 2012, never in my wildest imagination could I have foreseen the factual chain of events that I have imparted to you, the reader. These have left an indelible mark on my soul, but I stood firm against adversity in all its forms, my strength coming from the will to never give up. When it really mattered, I stepped up to the plate to help the two wonderful people who gave me a chance in the first place. Thank you, Mum and Dad, I feel blessed that you chose me for adoption, and I will love you both until the end of time itself; You truly have been my salvation.

Summary

Writing my factual life story has been both enjoyable and difficult; my parents rescued me when I was just a babe in arms and gave me the opportunity to flourish and achieve great things in life, the pinnacle being to share my experiences for you to read. I have certainly gone for it and left nothing out there, we only get one chance and should never look back with regret. To all my fellow adoptees, I trust that you have identified with this emotive subject that has played out in your own lives, and you are all safe and secure. With reference to my Mental Health issues, I am a living testament that adversity can be overcome; my lowest point was reached, and there appeared to be no way out, dark days indeed, but I found the will to survive and never ring that bell. If I have helped even just one person to navigate a pathway out of that rabbit hole, then well done to you.

On my return to Morden, it is much busier than when I grew up there, and the change in diversity is noticeable. However, the landmarks and infrastructure remain the same, just as I remember them. Walking down Woodland Way past our old house was emotional, and going full circle back to where my adventure began all those years ago has been such an inspiring journey.

Finally, my message to you is this: Always trust your instincts and retain self-belief, live life to the full and help other people.

www.ingramcontent.com/pod-product-compliance
Lightning Source LLC
Chambersburg PA
CBHW061223070526
44584CB00029B/3958